2000 MOST COMMON RUSSIAN WORDS IN CONTEXT

Get Fluent & Increase Your Russian Vocabulary with 2000 Russian Phrases

Russian Language Lessons

Lingo Mastery

ISBN: 9781698455143

FREE BOOK REVEALS THE 6 STEP BLUEPRINT THAT TOOK STUDENTS <u>FROM LANGUAGE LEARNERS TO FLUENT IN 3 MONTHS</u>

- **6 Unbelievable Hacks** that will accelerate your learning curve
- **Mind Training:** why memorizing vocabulary is easy
- **One Hack To Rule Them All:** This <u>secret nugget</u> will blow you away...

Head over to <u>**LingoMastery.com/hacks**</u>
and claim your free book now!

INTRODUCTION

Have you ever heard of Russian being one of the most complicated languages in the world? Well, we're not going to tell you it isn't – we're just offering a fun and efficient way to expand your vocabulary. We believe that learning a language should be associated with the pleasure of rewarding mental activity and the joy of discovering another culture rather than with the stress inherent to endless grammar drills.

Just remember that situation when you heard a foreigner say a few words in your language. Were you embarrassed by a wrong ending or some other mistake? No, you were happy they communicate with you in your mother tongue. The same thing is true for Russian-speaking people! Don't get us wrong – grammar is important but we don't want it to deprive you of the sense of achievement you get when you can express yourself in a language you're learning.

At the first sight the format of the book may resemble that of a dictionary, but it's far better than that. Unlike in a dictionary, we have sorted this book by the most frequently used words in the Russian language.

Just look at these three amazing stats found in a study done in 1964:

1. *Learning the first thousand (1000) most frequently used words of a language will allow you to understand 76.0% of all non-fiction writing, 79.6% of all fiction writing and an astounding 87.8% of all oral speech.*

2. *Learning the top two thousand (2000) most frequently used words*

will get you to 84% for non-fiction, 86.1% for fiction, and 92.7% for oral speech.

3. *Learning the top three thousand (3000) most frequently used words will get you to 88.2% for non-fiction, 89.6% for fiction, and 94.0% for oral speech.*

Look at these numbers once again and imagine what you could do once you've thoroughly read and practiced what it contains. We're providing you with two thousand of the most frequently used words – equivalent to an understanding of 92.7% of oral speech!

Of course these numbers will differ from language to language and from conversation to conversation but it's a good baseline.

We achieve this not only by giving you a long list of words; there must be context to allow the words to sink in, and we provide that. Each of the terms will be listed with its translation in English and two example sentences, one in each language, allowing you to study the use of each word in a common, accessible manner. We have ordered the terms according to their largest number of occurrences in common media, allowing you to begin with the simplest and most regularly-used words first before moving on to the less-used ones.

One more striking difference with a dictionary is the transcription. We know that the Russian Cyrillic alphabet has given many learners a hard time. We came up with a special way of transcribing words for you – the transcription is free from complicated signs in an Oxford dictionary style. It's a combination of transliteration and conventional signs used for transcription (read the transcription notes section).

Although we'd love to begin right away with helping you learn the vocabulary we've provided in this book, we've got a few tips and recommendations for getting the most out of this book.

Recommendations for readers of 2000 Most Common Words in Russian:

- An example you read can be transformed into an example you write. Why not try to practice the words we provide you with by using them in your own sentences? If you master this, you will not only be practicing your vocabulary, but also the use of verbs, nouns and sentences in general.

- Why limit yourself to 2000 words? While you're reading this book, you can always find 2000 more not-so-frequently-used words and practice them as well!

- Grab a partner or two and practice with them. Maybe it's your boyfriend/girlfriend, your roomie or even your parents; learning in groups is always easier than learning alone, and you can find somebody to practice your oral speech with. Just make sure they practice as hard as you do, since you don't want a lazy team-mate here!

- Use the vocabulary you've learned to write a story and share it with others to see how good (or bad) it is! Find help from a native speaker and let them help you improve your skills.

- In translation of words you may note that some words are separated by ',' and others are separated by ';'. Be attentive: the former one is for synonyms and the latter one is for completely different words.

Transcription notes

['] - used to mark the stressed syllable like in *'Мировой' [mira'voj]*. If the mark is missing, then there's only one syllable and it's obviously the stressed one.

['] - used to mark soft consonants like in *'Ударить' [u'darit']*

[ɛ] - sounds like 'a' in 'cat

[ə] - a neutral vowel, like the second 'e' in 'letter'

That is it! No super complex signs that look like Chinese hieroglyphs.

A Few Grammar Notes

As you probably know Russian is a language of declensions, endings and conjugations. To make life easier for you we've used only the initial forms of all the parts of speech except for a few words where it was impossible (there are comments provided in such cases). After all, before putting a verb in a second person singular form, for example, you need to know what it means, don't you?

However, there are a few grammatical categories that we found important to include. They relate to verbs only. You can come across the following commentaries: *perfective, impersonal* and *reflexive*.

The former one will help you to differentiate between the verbs with the same or almost the same translation like 'Сделать' ['zdelat'] – To do (perfective) and 'Делать' ['delat'] – To do.

The latter two will help you to understand the meaning better.

That is it! Go step by step – learn the words, practice them and you'll prepare a background for mastering grammar. But it's a different story.

1 - И [i] - *And*

Вчера она купила фрукты **и** овощи.
She bought some fruit **and** vegetables yesterday.

2 - В [v] - *In, on, at*

Маленький котёнок спрятался **в** подвале.
A little kitten hid **in** the basement.

3 - Не [nje] - *Not, no*

Я **не** люблю дождливую погоду.
I do **not** like rainy weather.

4 - Он [on] - *He*

Он очень хороший друг.
He is a very good friend.

5 - На [na] - *On, at*

Все книги стояли **на** столе.
All the books were lying **on** the table.

6 - Я [ja] - *I*

Я часто гуляю перед сном.
I often go for a walk before bedtime.

7 - Что [tchto] - *That*

Она не знала, **что** её мать больна.
She didn't know **that** her mother was ill.

8 - Тот [tot] - *That*

Тот парень у окна – мой брат.
That guy by the window is my brother.

9 - Быть [byt'] - *To be*

Непросто **быть** учителем.

It's not easy **to be** a teacher.

10 - C [s] - *With, from, off, since*

Могу я пойти **с** тобой?

May I go **with** you?

11 - А [a] - *And, but*

Его младший сын любит спорт, **а** старший интересуется искусством.

His younger son likes sports **and** the elder one is interested in art.

12 - Весь [vjes] - *All, whole*

Кто съел **весь** торт?

Who's eaten **all** the cake?

13 - Это ['ɛtə] - *It is, this is*

Это город, в котором выросла моя жена.

It's the town where my wife grew up.

14 - Как [kak] - *How, as*

Мы не знаем, **как** решить эту проблему.

We don't know **how** to solve this problem.

15 - Она [aˈna] - *She*

Я знаю, что **она** хочет на день рождения.

I know what **she** wants for her birthday.

16 - По [po] - *Along, over, till*

Друзья прогуливались **по** тихим улицам.

The friends were walking **along** the quiet streets.

17 - Но [no] - *But*

Солнце светит ярко, **но** на улице холодно.
The sun is shining brightly **but** it's cold outside.

18 - Они [aˈnji] - *They*

Они очень усердно учатся.
They study very hard.

19 - К [k] - **To, toward, by**

Не подходи близко **к** собаке – она может укусить.
Don't come close **to** the dog – it can bite.

20 - У [u] - *At, by, near*

Не стой **у** открытого окна, ты можешь простудиться!
Don't stand **by** the open window, you can catch a cold!

21 - Ты [ty] - **You (2nd person singular)**

Ты слишком поздно ложишься спать.
You go to bed too late.

22 - Из [ɪz] - *From, out of*

Я **из** Лондона.
I am **from** London.

23 - Мы [my] - *We*

Мы так рады видеть вас!
We are so happy to see you!

24 - За [za] - *Behind*

Что ты прячешь **за** спиной?
What are you hiding **behind** your back?

25 - Вы [vy] - You (2nd person plural or formal singular)

Дети, куда **вы** идёте?
Kids, where are **you** going?

26 - Так [tak] - *So, like that*

Я **так** сильно люблю тебя!
I love you **so** much!

27 - Же [zhe] - The same (in combination with 'такой', 'тот', 'то')

Со мной произошла **такая же** история.
The same story happened to me.

28 - От [ot] - *From, since*

Это сообщение **от** твоей сестры?
Is this message **from** your sister?

29 - Сказать [ska'zat'] - *To say, to tell*

Я даже не знаю, что **сказать**.
I don't even know what **to say**.

30 - Этот ['ɛtət] - *This, this one*

Тебе нравится **этот** фильм?
Do you like **this** movie?

31 - Который [ka'toryj] - *Which, that, who*

Это тест, **который** я провалил в прошлом году.
This is the test, **which** I failed last year.

32 - Мочь [motch] - Can, be able to (is never used in the initial form)

Я **могу** зайти завтра, если хочешь.
I **can** drop by tomorrow if you want.

33 - Человек [tchela'vek] - A person, a human being, a man

Её муж очень интересный **человек**.

Her husband is a very interesting **person**.

34 - О [o] - *About; oh*

Расскажи мне **о** себе.

Tell me **about** yourself.

35 - Один [a'din] - *One, alone, some*

Мне рассказал об этом **один** странный человек.

One strange man told me about it.

36 - Ещё [jestch'jo] - *Else, more, still*

Что-нибудь **ещё**?

Anything **else**?

37 - Бы [by] - A particle used in conditional or subjunctive patterns

Я **бы** не доверял им на твоём месте.

I **would** not trust them if I were you.

38 - Такой [ta'koj] - *Such*

Ты **такой** хороший игрок!

You're **such** a good player!

39 - Только ['tol'kə] - *Only, but*

Эти места **только** для пассажиров с детьми.

These seats are **only** for passengers with kids.

40 - Себя [seb'ja] - A reflexive pronoun (myself, yourself, herself etc.)

Она любит **себя** больше всего на свете.

She loves **herself** more than anything in the world.

41 - Своё [sva'jo] - A possessive pronoun common for all personal pronouns (my, his, her, its, our, your, their) and refers to the subject of the sentence. This form is for neuter nouns.

Он даже не помнит **своё** имя.

He doesn't even remember **his** name.

42 - Какой [ka'koj] - What, which, what kind of

Какой милый малыш!

What a cute baby!

43 - Когда [kag'da] - *When*

Когда ты вернулся?

When did you come back?

44 - Уже [u'zhɛ] - *Already*

Мы **уже** закончили работу.

We've **already** finished the work.

45 - Для [dlʲa] - *For*

Он ничего не сделал **для** общей победы.

He didn't do anything **for** the common victory.

46 - Вот [vot] - *Here (is/are)*

Вот ваше место.

Here is your seat.

47 - Кто [kto] - *Who*

Люди знают, **кто** виноват в трагедии.
People know **who** is to blame for the tragedy.

48 - Да [da] - *Yes*

Да, мы уверены, что он прав.
Yes, we're sure that he is right.

49 - Говорить [ɡava'rit'] - *To speak, to talk*

Ты мог бы **говорить** громче, пожалуйста?
Could you **speak** up, please?

50 - Год [ɡod] - *A year*

Это лучший **год** в моей жизни!
It's the best **year** of my life!

51 - Знать [znat'] - *To know*

Невозможно **знать** всё.
It's impossible **to know** everything.

52 - Мой [moj] - *My*

Это **мой** новый номер телефона, можешь удалить старый.
This is **my** new phone number; you can remove the old one.

53 - До [do] - *Before, till, up to*

До поступления в университет у неё было больше свободного времени.
Before entering the university, she had more free time.

54 - Или ['ili] - *Or*

Пара не могла решить, остаться дома **или** поехать за город.
The couple couldn't decide whether to stay at home **or** to go to the country.

11

55 - Если ['jeslı] - *If*

Если мы не поторопимся, то опоздаем на поезд.
If we don't hurry, we'll miss the train.

56 - Время ['vremja] - *Time*

Время нельзя остановить.
Time can't be stopped.

57 - Рука [ruka] - *A hand, an arm*

Мальчик крепко держал маму за **руку**.
The boy was firmly holding his mother by the **hand**.

58 - Нет [njet] - *No, there is no*

У меня совсем **нет** времени на спорт.
I have absolutely **no** time for sport.

59 - Самый ['samyj] - *The most*

Это **самый** захватывающий момент во всей книге.
It's **the most** exciting moment in the whole book.

60 - Ни [ni] - *Neither...nor, not*

Он не умеет играть **ни** в теннис, **ни** в гольф.
He can play **neither** tennis **nor** golf.

61 - Стать [stat'] - *To become, to stand*

Девушка всегда мечтала **стать** певицей.
The girl has always dreamt **to become** a singer.

62 - Большой [bal'shoj] - *Big, large*

Этот город слишком **большой** для меня.
This city is too **big** for me.

63 - Даже ['dazhe] - *Even*

Я **даже** не знаю, как благодарить вас!
I don't **even** know how to thank you!

64 - Другой [dru'goj] - **Other, another, different**

Вы можете предложить мне какой-нибудь **другой** цвет?
Can you offer me any **other** color?

65 - Наш [nash] - *Our*

Наш родной язык очень сложный.
Our mother tongue is very difficult.

66 - Свой [svoj] - **A possessive pronoun common for all personal pronouns (my, his, her, its, our, your, their) and refers to the subject of the sentence. This form is for masculine nouns.**

Я не могу вспомнить, где оставил **свой** зонт.
I can't remember where I left **my** umbrella.

67 - Ну [nu] - **Well (interjection)**

Ну, как тебе это платье?
Well, how do you like this dress?

68 - Под [pod] - *Under, below*

Она нашла потерянную серёжку **под** кроватью.
She found the lost earring **under** the bed.

69 - Где [gde] - *Where*

Не подскажете, **где** находится супермаркет?
Could you tell me **where** the supermarket is?

70 - Дело [d'jelə] - Business, case, matter

Извини, но это не твоё **дело**.

Sorry, but it's none of your **business**.

71 - Есть [jest'] - *To eat, there is/are*

Постарайся не **есть** после шести.

Try not **to eat** after 6 p.m.

72 - Сам [sam] - A reflexive pronoun emphasizing the ability to do something without any help, independently. Used for the pronouns 'He' and 'I' (If 'I' is masculine).

Он может готовить **сам**, но у него нет на это времени.

He can cook **himself**, but he doesn't have time for it.

73 - Раз [raz] - *A time*

Не забывай поливать этот цветок хотя бы один **раз** в неделю.

Remember to water this flower at least one **time** a week.

74 - Чтобы [ch'toby] - *So that, in order to*

Давай составим список покупок, **чтобы** ничего не забыть.

Let's make up a shopping list **so that** we don't forget anything.

75 - Два [dva] - *Two*

Есть **два** способа решить эту проблему.

There are **two** ways to solve this problem.

76 - Там [tam] - *There*

Посмотри, что это **там** такое?

Look, what is that over **there**?

77 - Чем [tchem] - *Than, rather*

Мои новые туфли более удобные, **чем** старые.
My old shoes are more comfortable **than** the old ones.

78 - Глаз [glaz] - *An eye*

У меня сильно болит правый **глаз**.
My right **eye** hurts badly.

79 - Жизнь [zhizn'] - *Life*

Она прожила сложную **жизнь**, но осталась очень доброй.
She lived a hard **life** but remained very kind.

80 - Первый ['pervyj] - *First*

Всегда сложно делать что-то в **первый** раз.
It's always difficult to do something for the **first** time.

81 - День [den'] - *Day, daytime*

Врачи рекомендуют начинать **день** со стакана чистой воды.
Doctors recommend starting the **day** with a glass of pure water.

82 - Тут [tut] - *Here*

Я помню, что оставил ключи **тут**, но не могу их найти.
I remember leaving the keys **here,** but I can't find them.

83 - Во [vo] - In, on, at (a variation of 'в' used before consonant clusters)

Во вторник состоится открытие международной выставки.
The opening of the international exhibition will take place **on** Tuesday.

84 - Ничто [nich'to] - *Nothing*

Ничто не остановит нас на пути к нашей цели.
Nothing will stop us on the way to our goal.

85 - Потом [pa'tom] - Then, afterwards, later

Идите прямо до перекрестка, а **потом** поверните налево.
Go straight ahead up to the crossroads and **then** turn left.

86 - Очень ['otchen'] - *Very, very much*

Тренер был **очень** разочарован результатами команды.
The coach was **very** disappointed with the team's results.

87 - Co [so] - With, off, from (a variation of 'c' used before consonant clusters)

Не мог бы ты остаться сегодня **со** мной?
Could you stay **with** me today?

88 - Хотеть [ha'tet'] - *To want*

Люди могут **хотеть** разного от жизни.
People may **want** different things from life.

89 - Ли [li] - *Whether, if*

Мне интересно, знают **ли** они правду.
I wonder **if** they know the truth.

90 - При [pri] - In the presence of, in the time of

Не говорите про путешествие **при** ней – это сюрприз.
Don't talk about the trip **in** her **presence**, it's a surprise.

91 - Голова [gala'va] - *Head*

Моя **голова** буквально раскалывается от этого шума.
My **head** is virtually splitting because of this noise.

92 - Надо ['nadə] - Need, must, (it is) necessary

Мне **надо** знать, сколько это займёт времени.
I **need** to know how much time it will take.

93 - Без [bez] - *Without*

Я не могу представить себе комнату **без** окон.
I can't imagine a room **without** windows.

94 - Видеть ['videt'] - *To see*

Со временем способность **видеть** ухудшается.
The ability **to see** is getting worse with time.

95 - Идти [i'ti] - *To go, to walk*

Нам лучше **идти** быстрее, если мы хотим успеть на встречу.
We'd better **go** faster if we want to be in time for the meeting.

96 - Теперь [te'per'] - *Now, in the present*

Теперь, когда ты всё объяснил, ситуация не кажется такой сложной.
Now that you explained everything the situation doesn't seem so difficult.

97 - Тоже ['tozhe] - *Also, too, as well*

Я **тоже** думаю, что эти перемены к лучшему.
I **also** think that these changes are for the better.

98 - Стоять [sta'jat'] - *To stand*

Нет никакой необходимости **стоять** в очереди: я уже купила билеты онлайн.
There is no need **to stand** in the queue: I have already bought the tickets online.

99 - Друг [drug] - *A friend*

Настоящий **друг** всегда рядом.
A true **friend** is always there for you.

100 - Дом [dom] - *A house, home*

Я хочу иметь большой частный **дом**.
I want to have a big private **house**.

101 - Сейчас [se'chas] - *Now, at the moment*

Сейчас она занята и не может подойти к телефону.
She is busy **now** and can't take the phone.

102 - Можно ['mozhnə] - *(one) May, (one) can, (it is) possible*

Можно мне воспользоваться твоим ноутбуком?
May I use your laptop?

103 - После ['posle] - *After*

Мой дедушка всегда спит **после** обеда.
My grandfather always sleeps **after** dinner.

104 - Слово ['slovo] - *A word*

Не могли бы вы объяснить мне, что значит это **слово**?
Could you explain to me what this **word** means?

105 - Здесь [zdes'] - *Here*

Купание **здесь** запрещено.
Swimming is forbidden **here**.

106 - Думать ['dumat'] - *To think, to suppose*

Я не могу **думать**, когда вокруг так шумно.
I can't **think** when it's so noisy around.

107 - Место ['mestə] - *A place, site*

Это очень мрачное **место**.
It's a very gloomy **place**.

108 – Спросить [spra'sit'] – *To ask, to inquire*

Лучше **спросить** его – он профессионал в этой области.
It's better **to ask** him – he's a professional in the field.

109 - Через ['tcherez] - *In (time), through, across*

Презентация будет готова **через** два дня.
The presentation will be ready **in** two days.

110 - Лицо [li'tso] - *A face*

Красивая душа лучше, чем красивое **лицо**.
A beautiful soul is better than a beautiful **face**.

111 - Что [tchto] - *What*

Я не знаю, **что** сказать, чтобы приободрить их.
I don't know **what** to say to cheer them up.

112 - Тогда [tag'da] - *Then, at that time*

Тогда они не знали, что скоро станут богаты.
They didn't know **then** that they would become rich soon.

113 - Ведь [ved'] - *After all, indeed*

Ведь мы не заставляли его принимать участие!
After all we didn't make him participate!

114 - Хороший [ha'roshyj] - *Good, fine*

Я уверен, это **хороший** знак.
I am sure it's a **good** sign.

115 - Каждый ['kazhdyj] - *Every, each*

Он занимается спортом **каждый** день.
He practices sport **every** day.

116 - Новый ['novyj] - *New*

Власти планируют построить здесь **новый** район.

The authorities are planning to build a **new** district here.

117 - Жить [zhyt'] - *To live, to reside*

Такие люди не заслуживают того, чтобы **жить**.

Such people don't deserve to **live**.

118 - Должный ['dolzhnyj] - *Due, proper*

Очень важно соблюдать **должный** порядок.

It's very important to maintain **duc** order.

119 - Смотреть [smat'ret'] - *To look, to watch*

Иногда сложно **смотреть** людям в глаза.

Sometimes it is difficult **to look** people in the eye.

120 - Почему [patche'mu] - *Why*

Я не могу понять, **почему** ты злишься на меня.

I can't understand **why** you're angry with me.

121 - Потому [pata'mu] - *Therefore, because of*

Сегодня у меня слишком много работы, **потому** я не смогу пойти на вечеринку.

I have too much work today; **therefore**, I won't be able to go to the party.

122 - Сторона [stara'na] - *A side; a party*

Эта **сторона** улицы более безопасная.

This **side** of the street is safer.

123 - Просто [p'rostə] - *Just; simply*

Я **просто** хотел убедиться, что всё в порядке.

I **just** wanted to make sure that everything is alright.

124 - Нога [na'ga] - *A leg, a foot*

Он немного хромает, потому что его правая **нога** короче левой.

He's a bit lame because his right **leg** is shorter than the left one.

125 - Сидеть [sidet'] - *To sit*

Маленькие дети не могут спокойно **сидеть**.
Little kids can't **sit** still.

126 - Понять [pan'jat'] - *To understand, to see (perfective)*

Иногда им очень трудно **понять** друг друга.
Sometimes it's very difficult for them to **understand** each other.

127 - Иметь [i'mjet'] - *To have*

Чтобы получить эту работу, нужно **иметь** хорошее образование.

To get this job one must **have** a good education.

128 - Конечный [ka'nechnyj] - *Final*

Руководство интересует **конечный** результат.
The management is interested in the **final** result.

129 - Делать ['delat'] - *To do; to make*

Я не знаю, что **делать** в такой ситуации.
I don't know what **to do** in such a situation.

130 - Вдруг [vdrug] - *Suddenly*

Вдруг тёмная туча закрыла солнце.
Suddenly a dark cloud covered the sun.

131 - Над [nad] - *Above, over*

Высоко **над** крышами быстро летали птицы.
Birds were quickly flying high **above** the roofs.

132 - Взять [vzjat'] - *To take*

Можешь **взять** все, что тебе нравится.
You can **take** anything you like.

133 - Никто [nik'to] - *Nobody*

Никто не любит плохого отношения.
Nobody likes bad attitude.

134 - Сделать ['zdelat'] - *To do, to make (perfective form)*

Что можно **сделать**, чтобы помочь им?
What can **be done** to help them?

135 - Дверь [dver'] - *A door*

Эта **дверь** ведёт в большую комнату.
This **door** leads to a big room.

136 - Перед ['pered] - *In front of, before*

Он выступил с речью **перед** большой аудиторией.
He made a speech **in front of** a large audience.

137 - Нужный ['nuzhnyj] - *Necessary, needed*

Рабочий долго не мог найти нужный инструмент.
He couldn't find the **necessary** tool for a long time.

138 - Понимать [pani'mat'] - *To understand, to see*

Научись **понимать** людей вокруг себя.
Learn **to understand** people around you.

139 - Казаться [ka'zatsa] - *To seem*

Молодой человек не хотел **казаться** слабым.
The young man didn't want **to seem** weak.

140 - Работа [ra'bota] - *Work; job*

Ведётся **работа** над восстановлением здания.
The **work** on the restoration of the building is being carried out.

141 - Три [tri] - *Three*

Мне нужно **три** копии этого документа.
I need **three** copies of this document.

142 - Ваш [vash] - *Your, yours (2ⁿᵈ person plural or 2ⁿᵈ person singular formal)*

Покажите **ваш** паспорт, пожалуйста.
Show **your** passport, please.

143 - Уж [uzh] - *Emphatic particle*

Я никода не забуду твоих слов, **уж** это точно!
I'll never forget your words, that's **for sure**!

144 - Земля [zem'lja] - *Earth; land*

Земля снабжает нас всем необходимым.
The **Earth** provides us with everything we need.

145 - Конец [ka'nets] - *An end; ending*

Конец истории был неожиданным.
The **end** of the story was unexpected.

146 - Несколько ['neskalkə] - *A few, some*

Мне нужно **несколько** надёжных людей.
I need **a few** reliable people.

147 - Час [tchas] - *An hour*

Остался всего один **час** до конца представления.
There's only one **hour** left before the end of the performance.

148 - Голос ['goləs] - *A voice*

Мне всегда нравился её мягкий **голос**.
I've always liked her soft **voice**.

149 - Город ['gorəd] - *A city, a town*

В этот **город** всегда приятно возвращаться.
It's always pleasant to go back to this **city**.

150 - Последний [pas'lednij] - *Last, latest*

Последний раз мы виделись три года назад.
Last time we saw each other three years ago.

151 - Пока [pa'ka] - *While; for now*

Пока меня не будет, за домом присмотрит моя сестра.
While I'm away my sister will look after the house.

152 - Хорошо [hara'sho] - *Well*

Она достаточно **хорошо** знает русскую литературу.
She knows Russian literature quite **well**.

153 - Давать [da'vat'] - *To give*

Я не могу **давать** советы в такой ситуации.
I can't **give** advice in such a situation.

154 - Вода [va'da] - *Water*

Вода – это источник жизни на земле.
Water is the source of life on earth.

155 - Более ['boleje] - *More, more than*

Считается, что британцы **более** консервативны, чем американцы.

It's considered that the British are **more** conservative than the Americans.

156 - Хотя [ha'tja] - *Although, though*

Мы хорошо погуляли, **хотя** было холодно.

We had a nice walk, **although** it was cold.

157 - Всегда [vseg'da] - *Always*

Я **всегда** бегаю по утрам.

I **always** go jogging in the morning.

158 - Второй [vta'roj] - *Second*

Второй вариант проекта был более успешным.

The **second** variant of the project was more successful.

159 - Куда [ku'da] - *Where (to)*

Куда мне можно поставить свои вещи?

Where can I put my things?

160 - Пойти [paj'ti] - *To go (to)*

Не хочешь ли ты **пойти** в кино?

Would you like **to go** to the cinema?

161 - Стол [stol] - *A table*

Накрой на **стол**, пожалуйста.

Lay the **table**, please.

162 - Ребёнок [reb'jonǝk] - *A child, a kid*

Этот **ребёнок** очень плохо себя ведёт.

This **child** behaves very badly.

163 - Увидеть [u'videt'] - *To see (perfective)*

Я хочу **увидеть** Большой Каньон.
I want **to see** The Grand Canyon.

164 - Сила ['sila] - *Power, strength*

Нужна большая **сила** воли, чтобы бросить курить.
A strong **power** of will is needed to give up smoking.

165 - Отец [a'tets] - *Father*

Отец уделял много времени нашему воспитанию.
Father devoted a lot of time to our upbringing.

166 - Женщина ['zhenschina] - *A woman*

Кажется, эта **женщина** идеальная.
It seems this **woman** is perfect.

167 - Машина [ma'shina] - *A car; machine*

Его новая **машина** очень дорогая, но надёжная.
His new **car** is very expensive but reliable.

168 - Случай ['sluchaj] - *A case*

Это самый сложный **случай** в моей карьере.
It's the most complicated **case** in my career.

169 - Ночь [notch] - *Night*

Ночь была удивительно тёплой и светлой.
The **night** was surprisingly warm and light.

170 - Сразу ['srazu] - *At once*

Я **сразу** понял, что это ложь.
I understood **at once** that it was a lie.

171 - Мир [mir] - *A world; peace*

Весь **мир** следит за этими событиями.
The whole **world** is following these events.

172 - Совсем [sav'sem] - *At all*

Мы **совсем** не возражаем против таких перемен.
We don't mind such changes **at all**.

173 - Остаться [as'tatsa] - *To stay, to remain*

К сожалению, вам придётся **остаться** дома.
Unfortunately, you'll have **to stay** at home.

174 - Об [ob] - *About (before vowels)*

Я не могу ничего сказать **об** остальных актёрах.
I can't say anything **about** the rest of the actors.

175 - Вид [vid] - *Kind; look; view*

Какой твой любимый **вид** спорта?
What is your favorite **kind** of sport?

176 - Выйти ['vyjti] - *To go out, to exit*

Наконец, им удалось **выйти** из лабиринта.
At last, they managed **to go out** of the labyrinth.

177 - Дать [dat'] - *To give (perfective)*

Что они могут **дать** нам взамен?
What can they **give** us in return?

178 - Работать [ra'botat'] - *To work*

Врачам часто приходится **работать** сверхурочно.
Doctors often have **to work** overtime.

179 - Любить [lju'bit'] - *To love, to like*

Такие люди неспособны **любить**.
Such people aren't able **to love**.

180 - Старый ['staryj] - *Old*

Старый рынок популярен среди туристов.
The **old** market is popular with tourists.

181 - Почти [pach'ti] - *Almost*

Они женаты **почти** два года.
They've been married for **almost** two years.

182 - Ряд [rjad] - *A row; a range*

Билеты в первый **ряд** уже проданы.
The tickets in the first **row** are sold already.

183 - Оказаться [aka'zatsa] - *To turn out; to find oneself*

Это лекарство может **оказаться** опасным.
This medicine can **turn out** to be dangerous.

184 - Начало [na'chalə] - *Beginning, start*

Начало пути показалось нам немного трудным.
The **beginning** of the way seemed a bit hard to us.

185 - Твой [tvoj] - Your (2nd person singular)

Твой доклад очень подробный.
Your report is very detailed.

186 - Вопрос [vap'ros] - *A question; matter*

Можно задать тебе личный **вопрос**?
May I ask you a personal **question**?

187 - Много ['mnogə] - *Many, much, a lot of*

У меня сегодня слишком **много** дел.
I have too **many** things to do today.

188 - Война [vaj'na] - *A war*

Любая **война** – это катастрофа.
Any **war** is a disaster.

189 - Снова ['snova] - *Again*

Когда мы встретимся **снова**?
When will we meet **again**?

190 - Ответить [at'vjetit'] - *To answer, to reply*

Постарайся **ответить** на этот вопрос честно.
Try **to answer** this question honestly.

191 - Между ['mezhdu] - *Between*

Какова разница **между** этими словами?
What is the difference **between** these words?

192 - Подумать [pa'dumat'] - *To think (perfective)*

Мне нужно хорошо **подумать**, прежде чем я смогу ответить.
I need **to think** well before I'll be able to answer.

193 - Опять [ap'jat'] - *Again*

Он **опять** сделал ту же самую ошибку.
He made the same mistake **again**.

194 - Белый ['belyj] - *White*

Белый костюм не сочетается с этими зелёными туфлями.
A **white** suit doesn't match these green shoes.

195 - Деньги ['djengi] - *Money*

Нельзя купить счастье за **деньги**.
You can't buy happiness for **money**.

196 - Значить ['znatchit'] - *To mean*

Что бы это могло **значить**?
What could it **mean**?

197 - Про [pro] - *About*

Она и думать не могла **про** развод.
She couldn't even think **about** a divorce.

198 - Лишь [lish'] - *Just, only*

Это **лишь** слова – не принимай близко к сердцу.
These are **just** words – don't take it close to heart.

199 - Минута [mi'nuta] - *A minute*

Иногда одна **минута** может длиться очень долго.
Sometimes one **minute** can last very long.

200 - Жена ['zhena] - *A wife*

Его **жена** прекрасно выглядела на приеме.
His **wife** looked wonderful at the reception.

201 - Посмотреть [pasmatr'jet'] - *To look (perfective); to see*

Мне нужно самой **посмотреть** на эти файлы.
I need **to look** at these files myself.

202 - Правда ['pravda] - *Truth*

Правда всегда выходит наружу.
The **truth** always comes out.

203 - Главный ['glavnyj] - *Main, chief*

Главный герой пьесы – одинокий инженер.
The **main** character of the play is a lonely engineer.

204 - Страна [stra'na] - *A country*

Вся **страна** ждёт результатов голосования.
The whole **country** is waiting for the results of the vote.

205 - Свет [svet] - *Light*

Не забудь выключить **свет**!
Don't forget to turn off the **light**!

206 - Ждать [zhdat'] - *To wait*

Я просто не могу больше **ждать**.
I just can't **wait** anymore.

207 - Мать [mat'] - *A mother*

Мать невесты была строгой женщиной.
The bride's **mother** was a strict woman.

208 - Будто ['budtə] - *As if; allegedly*

Она так устала, **будто** работала весь день.
She was so tired **as if** she had worked the whole day.

209 - Никогда [nikag'da] - *Never*

Мы **никогда** не используем пластиковые пакеты.
We **never** use plastic bags.

210 - Товарищ [ta'varistch] - *Comrade; a friend, a mate*

В СССР люди называли друг друга «**товарищ**».
In the USSR people used to call each other '**comrade**'.

211 - Дорога [da'roga] - *A road, a way*

Эта **дорога** ведёт к лесу.
This **road** leads to the forest.

212 - Однако [ad'nakə] - *However, yet*

Однако никто не поддержал мою идею.
However, nobody supported my idea.

213 - Лежать [lje'zhat'] - *To lie*

Сегодня вечером я хочу **лежать** на диване и смотреть телевизор.
Tonight, I want **to lie** on the sofa and to watch TV.

214 - Именно ['imennə] - *Exactly, just*

Что **именно** ты имеешь ввиду?
What **exactly** do you mean?

215 - Окно [ak'no] - *A window*

Закрой **окно**, пожалуйста, уже холодно.
Close the **window**, please, it's cold already.

216 - Никакой [nika'koj] - *No, none, not any*

Никакой аргумент не изменит их решение.
No argument will change their decision.

217 - Найти [naj'ti] - *To find*

Я не могу **найти** свои коричневые брюки.
I can't **find** my brown trousers.

218 - Писать [pi'sat'] - *To write*

Я не умею **писать** длинные письма.
I can't **write** long letters.

219 - Комната ['komnata] - *A room*

Детская **комната** всегда в беспорядке.
The children's **room** is always a mess.

220 - Москва [Mosc'va] - *Moscow*

Москва – столица Российской Федерации.
Moscow is the capital of the Russian Federation.

221 - Часть [tchast'] - *A part*

Это только первая **часть** концерта.
It's only the first **part** of the concert.

222 - Вообще [voobs'tche] - *In general, generally*

Вообще я не фанат триллеров.
In general, I'm not a fan of thrillers.

223 - Книга ['kniga] - *A book*

Книга – лучший подарок.
A **book** is the best present.

224 - Маленький ['maljenkyj] - *Small, little*

Их дом **маленький**, но очень уютный.
Their house is **small** but very cozy.

225 - Улица ['ulitsa] - *A street*

Эта **улица** только для пешеходов.
This **street** is for pedestrians only.

226 - Решить [re'shit'] - *To decide*

Компания не может **решить**, какого кандидата выбрать.
The company can't **decide** which candidate to choose.

227 - Далеко [dale'ko] - *Far away*

Все её родственники живут **далеко**.
All her relatives live **far away**.

228 - Душа [du'sha] - *A soul*

Душа – самое дорогое, что есть у человека.
A soul is the most precious thing a person has.

229 - Чуть ['tchut'] - *A bit, slightly; barely*

Свадебное платье стоило **чуть** дороже, чем мы ожидали.
The wedding dress cost **a bit** more than we expected.

230 - Вернуться [ver'nuts'ja] - *To return, to come back*

Мы планируем **вернуться** до полуночи.
We are planning **to return** before midnight.

231 - Утро ['utrə] - *Morning*

То осеннее **утро** было туманным и холодным.
That autumn **morning** was foggy and cold.

232 - Некоторый ['nekətəryj] - *Some*

В его словах есть **некоторый** скрытый смысл.
There's **some** hidden sense in his words.

233 - Считать [schi'tat'] - *To consider; to count*

Эту книгу уже можно **считать** классикой.
You can already **consider** this book to be a classic one.

234 - Сколько ['skol'kə] - *How many, how much*

Сколько гостей вы пригласили на вечеринку?
How many guests have you invited to the party?

235 - Помнить ['pomnit'] - *To remember*

Мы всегда будем **помнить** героизм наших солдат.
We'll always **remember** the heroism of our soldiers.

236 - Вечер ['vetcher'] - *Evening*

Мы провели незабываемый романтический **вечер**.
We spent an unforgettable romantic **evening**.

237 - Пол [pol] - *Floor*

Она **уронила** кошелёк на пол и не заметила этого.
She **dropped** the purse on the floor and didn't notice it.

238 - Таки [ta'ki] - *Still, in spite of, after all*

Она **таки** простила своего врага.
Still, she forgave her enemy.

239 - Получить [palu'tchit'] - *To get, to receive*

Наш менеджер надеется **получить** повышение.
Our manager hopes **to get** a raise.

240 - Народ [na'rod] - *People, nation*

Политики часто обманывают **народ**.
Politicians often deceive **people**.

241 - Плечо [ple'tcho] - *A shoulder*

Он вывихнул **плечо** во время тренировки.
He dislocated his **shoulder** during a workout.

242 - Хоть ['hot'] - *Though, in spite of*

Хоть она и прожила в Испании десять лет, она не знает языка.
Though she's been living in Spain for ten years, she doesn't know the language.

243 - Сегодня [se'godnja] - *Today*

Сегодня мой брат празднует юбилей.
Today my brother celebrates his anniversary.

244 - Бог [bog] - *God*

Только **Бог** может нам помочь!
Only **God** can help us!

245 - Вместе [v'mestje] - *Together*

Это очень дружная семья: они все делают **вместе**.
It's a very close-knit family – they do everything **together**.

246 - Взгляд [vzgljad] - *View; glance, look*

На мой **взгляд**, этих денег недостаточно.
In my **view** this money is not enough.

247 - Ходить [ha'dit'] - *To walk, to go*

После операции он снова сможет **ходить**.
After the surgery he'll be able **to walk** again.

248 - Зачем [za'tchem] - *What for, why*

Зачем тебе нужны эти специи?
What do you need these spices **for**?

249 - Советский [sa'vjetskij] - *Soviet*

Советский Союз был основан в 1922.
The **Soviet** Union was founded in 1922.

250 - Русский ['ruskij] - *Russian*

Русский один из самых сложных языков.
Russian is one of the most difficult languages.

251 - Бывать [by'vat'] - *To be at, to visit*

Жаль, что я не могу **бывать** у бабушки чаще.
I wish I could **be** at my granny's more often.

252 - Полный ['polnyj] - *Full, complete*

Это ещё не **полный** потенциал оборудования.
It's not yet the **full** potential of the equipment.

253 - Прийти [prij'ti] - *To come to*

Они извинились за то, что не смогут **прийти** на похороны.
They apologized for not being able **to come** to the funeral.

254 - Палец ['palets] - *A finger; a toe*

Повар порезал себе **палец** пока чистил картофель.
The cook cut his **finger** while he was peeling potatoes.

255 - Россия [ra'sija] - *Russia*

Россия богата природными ресурсами.
Russia is rich in natural resources.

256 - Любой [lu'boj] - *Any*

Любой другой человек испугался бы, но не мой отец.
Any other person would get scared but not my father.

257 - История [is'torija] - *History; a story*

История хранит много секретов.
History keeps lots of secrets.

258 - Наконец [naka'njets] - *At last, in the end*

Наконец, стороны пришли к соглашению.
At last the parties reached an agreement.

259 - Мысль ['mysl'] - *A thought*

Это неожиданная, но очень полезная **мысль**.

It's an unexpected but a very useful **thought**.

260 - Узнать [uz'nat'] - *To recognize; to find out*

Я не смог **узнать** её из-за тёмных очков.

I couldn't **recognize** her because of the dark glasses.

261 - Назад [na'zad] - *Back, backwards*

Путешественникам не хотелось поворачивать **назад**.

The travellers didn't want to turn **back**.

262 - Общий ['obstchij] - *Common, public*

У них есть **общий** недостаток – они слишком много
разговаривают.

They have a **common** drawback – they talk too much.

263 - Заметить [za'metit'] - *To notice*

Дети не могли не **заметить**, что мама чем-то расстроена.

The children couldn't help but **notice** that their mother was upset
with something.

264 - Словно ['slovnə] - *Like, as if*

Я так хорошо себя чувствую, **словно** стала на пять лет моложе.

I feel so good, **like** I'm five years younger.

265 - Прошлый ['proshlyj] - *Last, past*

В прошлый раз мы отослали слишком мало приглашений.

Last time we sent too few invitations.

266 - Уйти [uj'ti] - *To leave, to go away*

Очень грубо с твоей стороны **уйти** не попрощавшись.

It's very rude of you **to leave** without saying goodbye.

267 - Известный [iz'vesnyj] - *Known, familiar*

Хорошо **известный** писатель дал интервью читателям.
A well-**known** writer gave an interview to the readers.

268 - Давно [dav'no] - *Long ago*

Интересно, как **давно** они купили новую машину.
I wonder how **long ago** they bought a new car.

269 - Слышать ['slyshat'] - *To hear*

Родители говорили громко, и дети могли **слышать** каждое слово.
The parents were talking loudly and the children could **hear** every word.

270 - Слушать ['slushat'] - *To listen to*

Я не могу больше **слушать** эту чепуху!
I can't **listen** to this nonsense anymore!

271 - Бояться [ba'jatsa] - *To fear, to be afraid of*

Не нужно **бояться** плохих снов.
One shouldn't **fear** bad dreams.

272 - Сын [syn] - *A son*

Мой **сын** окончил университет в этом году.
My **son has** graduated from University this year.

273 - Нельзя [nelzj'a] - *One cannot, it's prohibited*

Здесь **нельзя** пользоваться мобильным.
One **cannot** use a mobile here.

274 - Прямо [pr'jamə] - *Straight; openly*

Группа шла **прямо**, а у почты повернула направо.
The group was going **straight** ahead and turned right at the post office.

275 - Долго ['dolgə] - *Long (adv)*

Я хочу, чтобы мои родители жили **долго**.
I want my parents to live **long**.

276 - Быстрый ['bystryj] - *Quick, fast*

Мне нужен **быстрый** ответ.
I need a **quick** answer.

277 - Лес ['les] - *Forest, woods*

Осенью мы часто ходим в **лес** за грибами.
In autumn we often go to the **forest** to pick up mushrooms.

278 - Похожий [pa'hozhyj] - *Similar, alike*

В детстве у меня был **похожий** кукольный домик.
In my childhood I had a **similar** doll house.

279 - Пора [pa'ra] - *It is time; a season*

Пора принять окончательное решение.
It is time to make a final decision.

280 - Пять [p'jat'] - *Five*

Сегодня моей племяннице исполнилось **пять**.
My niece turned **five** today.

281 - Глядеть [g'ljadet'] - *To look, to watch*

Собака могла часами **глядеть** из окна, ожидая возвращения хозяина.

The dog could **look** out of the window for hours waiting for the master's return.

282 - Оно [a'no] - It (third-person neuter singular pronoun)

Не ешь это яблоко – **оно** гнилое.
Don't eat this apple – **it** is rotten.

283 - Сесть ['sest] - *To sit down*

В этой комнате негде **сесть**.
There's nowhere **to sit down** in this room.

284 - Имя ['imja] - *A name*

Это **имя** очень необычное для нашей страны.
This **name** is very unusual for our country.

285 - Ж [zh] - *A particle that makes an objection by pointing to an obvious fact - after all, but (A shorter form of 'же')*

Почему ты мне не веришь? Я **ж** говорю правду!
Why don't you believe me? **After all** I'm telling the truth!

286 - Разговор [razga'vor] - *A talk, a conversation*

У меня был очень неприятный **разговор** с начальством.
I had a very unpleasant **talk** with the management.

287 - Тело ['telə] - *A body*

Её **тело** просто божественное!
Her **body** is just divine!

41

288 - Молодой [mala'doj] - *Young*

Кто этот **молодой** человек на фото?
Who's this **young** man in the photo?

289 - Стена [ste'na] - *A wall*

Великая Китайская **стена** – это уникальное сооружение.
The Great Chinese **Wall** is a unique construction.

290 - Красный ['krasnyj] - *Red*

Красный – это цвет страсти.
Red is the color of passion.

291 - Читать [tchi'tat'] - *To read*

Мой младший брат может **читать** часами.
My younger brother can **read** for hours.

292 - Право ['pravə] - *Right; law*

Каждый гражданин имеет **право** голосовать.
Every citizen has the **right** to vote.

293 - Старик [sta'rik] - *An old man*

«**Старик** и море» – одно из лучших произведений Хемингуэя.
"The **Old Man** and the Sea" is one of the best works by Hemingway.

294 - Ранний ['rannij] - *Early (Adj)*

У нас был спокойный **ранний** завтрак.
We had a peaceful **early** breakfast.

295 - Хотеться [ha'tetsa] - *To want (impersonal)*

Тебе должно **хотеться** большего от жизни.
You must **want** more from life.

296 - Мама ['mama] - *Mama, mummy*

Его первым словом было «**мама**».
His first word was "**mama**".

297 - Оставаться [asta'vatsa] - *To remain, to stay*

Безопасность будет **оставаться** твоей обязанностью.
Security will **remain** your responsibility.

298 - Высокий ['vysokij] - *Tall, high*

Он не достаточно **высокий**, чтобы играть в баскетбол.
He's not tall enough to play basketball.

299 - Путь [put'] - *Way, path*

Тебе нужно найти свой **путь** развития.
You should find your own **way** of development.

300 - Поэтому [pa'ɛtəmu] - *Therefore, that is why*

Я простудился, **поэтому** не поехал в горы.
I caught a cold, **therefore** I didn't go to the mountains.

301 - Совершенно [saver'shennə] - *Absolutely, completely*

Этот прибор **совершенно** бесполезен.
This device is **absolutely** useless.

302 - Кроме ['krome] - *Except; besides*

Все, **кроме** меня, сдали тест.
Everyone, **except** me, passed the test.

303 - Тысяча ['tysjacha] - *A thousand*

У неё была **тысяча** причин бросить работу.
She had a **thousand** reasons to quit her job.

304 - Месяц ['mesjats] - *A month; moon*

Декабрь – это зимний **месяц**.
December is a winter **month**.

305 - Брать [brat'] - *To take*

Я не советую тебе **брать** кредит.
I don't recommend you **to take** a loan.

306 - Написать [napi'sat'] - *To write*

Автору удалось **написать** книгу за несколько месяцев.
The author managed **to write** the book in a few months.

307 - Целый ['tselyj] - *Whole; entire*

Ученый потратил **целый** год на это изобретение.
The scientist spent a **whole** year on this invention.

308 - Огромный [ag'romnyj] - *Huge, vast*

У этой технологии **огромный** потенциал.
This technology has a **huge** potential.

309 - Начинать [natchi'nat'] - *To start, to begin*

Мы не будем **начинать** конференцию без него.
We won't **start** the conference without him.

310 - Спина [spi'na] - *A back*

После вчерашней работы в саду у меня сильно болит **спина**.
My **back** hurts badly after yesterday's work in the garden.

311 - Настоящий [nasta'jastchij] - *Real, true; present*

Этот пожарный – **настоящий** герой.
This firefighter is a **real** hero.

312 - Пусть [pust'] - Let + subject + the verb

Пусть все твои дни будут счастливыми!
Let all your days be happy!

313 - Язык [ja'zyk] - *Language; tongue*

Нужно много терпения, чтобы выучить иностранный **язык**.
A lot of patience is needed to learn a foreign **language**.

314 - Точно ['tochnə] - *Exactly, definitely*

Я **точно** знаю, что делать.
I know **exactly** what to do.

315 - Среди [sre'di] - *Among*

Он самый опытный работник **среди** своих коллег.
He's the most experienced worker **among** his colleagues.

316 - Чувствовать ['tchustvəvət'] - *To feel*

Ты не должна **чувствовать** себя виноватой в том, что произошло.
You shouldn't **feel** guilty for what's happened.

317 - Сердце ['sertse] - *Heart*

Это предательство разбило его **сердце**.
This betrayal broke his **heart**.

318 - Вести [ves'ti] - *To lead*

Я уверен, что эта дорога не может **вести** в город.
I'm sure this road can't **lead** to the city.

319 - Иногда [inag'da] - *Sometimes*

Иногда моя сестра ведёт себя достаточно эгоистично.
My sister behaves quite selfishly **sometimes**.

320 - Мальчик ['mal'chik] - A boy

Мой племянник очень активный **мальчик**.

My nephew is a very active **boy**.

321 - Успеть [us'pet'] - To have time, to make it, to be in time for

Мы можем не **успеть** увидеть все достопримечательности.

We may not **have time to** see all the sights.

322 - Небо ['nebə] - *Sky*

Смотреть на звёздное **небо** – это очень романтично.

Watching the starry **sky** is very romantic.

323 - Живой [zhi'voj] - *Live, alive, living*

Это был **живой** концерт классической музыки.

That was a **live** concert of classical music.

324 - Смерть ['smert'] - *Death*

Смерть президента стала шоком для всей страны.

The president's **death** came as a shock for the whole country.

325 - Продолжать [pradal'zhat'] - *To continue, to go on*

Я буду **продолжать** помогать этой семье.

I'll **continue** to help this family.

326 - Девушка ['devushka] - *A girl*

Это **девушка** моей мечты.

It's the **girl** of my dreams.

327 - Образ ['obraz] - *Image; style*

Образ матери был центральным в его книгах.

The **image** of a mother was the central one in his books.

328 - Ко [ko] - To; towards (variant of 'к' used before consonants)

Отношение профессора **ко** мне очень изменилось.

The professor's attitude **to** me changed a lot.

329 - Забыть [za'byt'] - *To forget*

Как ты мог **забыть** о годовщине нашей свадьбы?

How could you **forget** about our wedding anniversary?

330 - Вокруг [vak'rug] - *Around, round*

Всё **вокруг** было покрыто снегом.

Everything **around** was covered in snow.

331 - Письмо [pis''mo] - *A letter; writing*

Почтальон потерял моё **письмо**.

The postman lost my **letter**.

332 - Власть ['vlast'] - *Power, authority*

У королевы только номинальная **власть**.

The Queen only has nominal **power**.

333 - Чёрный ['tchjornyj] - *Black*

Чёрный считается цветом деловой одежды.

Black is considered to be the color of business clothes.

334 - Пройти [praj'ti] - *To pass, to pass by*

Должен **пройти** по крайней мере год, прежде чем ситуация изменится.

At least a year should **pass** before the situation changes.

335 - Появиться [paja'vitsa] - *To appear; to show up*

Это жирное пятно не могло **появиться** здесь само.

This greasy stain couldn't **appear** here by itself.

336 - Воздух ['vozduh] - *Air*

Заводы загрязняют **воздух**.

Factories contaminate **the air**.

337 - Разный ['raznyj] - *Different; varied*

У них **разный** цвет лица.

They have **different** complexion.

338 - Выходить [vyho'dit'] - *To go out*

Я не рекомендую тебе **выходить** из дома – там идёт сильный дождь.

I don't recommend you **to go out** of the house – it's raining heavily there.

339 - Просить [pra'sit'] - *To ask; to request*

Капитан был слишком гордым, чтобы **просить** о помощи.

The captain was too proud to **ask** for help.

340 - Брат [brat] - *A brother*

Его **брат** будет моим соперником в завтрашнем матче.

His **brother** will be my opponent in tomorrow's match.

341 - Собственный ['sobstvenyj] - *One's own*

Она открыла свой **собственный** бизнес.

She started her **own** business.

342 - Отношение [atna'shenije] - *Attitude*

Его **отношение** к учёбе заслуживает уважения.

His **attitude** to studies deserves respect.

343 - Затем [za'tem] - *Then*

На первом свидании мы сходили в кафе, а **затем** прогулялись по парку.

On the first date we went to a cafe and **then** walked through the park.

344 - Пытаться [py'tatsa] - *To try*

Не нужно **пытаться** обмануть меня – я уже всё знаю.

You shouldn't **try** to deceive me – I know everything already.

345 - Показать [paka'zat'] - *To show*

Мне не терпится **показать** тебе, что я купил.

I can't wait **to show** you what I bought.

346 - Вспомнить [vs'pomnit'] - *To recollect, to remember*

Бабушка не могла **вспомнить**, где видела этого человека.

Grandmother couldn't **recollect** where she'd seen that man.

347 - Система [sis'tema] - *A system*

Ни одна политическая **система** не идеальна.

No political **system** is perfect.

348 - Четыре [tche'tyre] - *Four*

Мы звонили им **четыре** раза – ответа нет.

We called them **four** times – no answer.

349 - Квартира [kvar'tira] - *Apartment, flat*

Наша **квартира** находится на пятом этаже.

Our **apartment** is on the fifth floor.

350 - Держать [der'zhat'] - *To hold; to keep*

Я не могу больше **держать** эту тяжёлую сумку.
I can't **hold** this heavy bag anymore.

351 - Также ['takzhe] - *Also, too, as well*

Я **также** хочу обратить ваше внимание на проблемы медицины.
I **also** want to pay your attention to the problems of medicine.

352 - Любовь [lju'bov'] - *Love*

Я не уверен, что это **любовь**.
I'm not sure it's **love**.

353 - Солдат [sal'dat] - *A soldier*

Любой **солдат** скучает по дому.
Any **soldier** misses his home.

354 - Откуда [at'kuda] - *Where from*

Откуда эти апельсины?
Where are these oranges **from**?

355 - Чтоб [tchtob] - So that, in order to, so as to (a short variant of 'чтобы')

Я оставила тебе записку, **чтоб** ты знал, где я.
I left you a note **so that** you know where I am.

356 - Называть [nazy'vat'] - *To call; to name*

Я предпочитаю **называть** людей по имени.
I prefer **to call** people by the name.

357 - Третий ['tretij] - *Third*

Третий вопрос оказался самым простым.
The **third** question turned out to be the easiest one.

358 - Хозяин [ha'zjain] - *An owner; a master*

Кто **хозяин** этой роскошной квартиры?
Who's the **owner** of this luxury flat?

359 - Вроде ['vrode] - *Like, such as, kind of*

Люди **вроде** него раздражают меня.
People **like** him irritate me.

360 - Уходить [uha'dit'] - *To leave*

Нам совсем не хотелось **уходить** с вечеринки.
We didn't want **to leave** the party at all.

361 - Подойти [padaj'ti] - *To come to, to approach*

Не мог бы ты **подойти** ближе ко мне – я плохо слышу.
Could you **come** closer **to** me – I don't hear well.

362 - Поднять [padn'jat'] - *To raise*

Учитель попросил учеников **поднять** руки, если они согласны с высказыванием.
The teacher asked the students to **raise** their hands if they agreed with the expression.

363 - Особенно [a'sobennə] - *Especially*

На приёме мне **особенно** понравилась музыка.
At the reception I **especially** liked the music.

364 - Спрашивать [sp'rashivat'] - *To ask about*

Очень невежливо **спрашивать** о личных вопросах.
It's very impolite **to ask about** personal matters.

365 - Начальник [na'chal'nik] - *A boss, a chief*

Наш **начальник** на удивление понимающий человек.
Our **boss** is a surprisingly understanding person.

366 - Оба ['oba] - Both (for masculine nouns])

Оба примера отлично подходят для описания ситуации.
Both examples suit great to describe the situation.

367 - Бросить ['brosit'] - *To throw; to give up*

Как ты мог **бросить** камень прямо в окно?
How could you **throw** a stone right at the window?

368 - Школа [sh'kola] - *A school*

Эта элитная **школа** принимает только лучших учеников.
This elite **school** accepts only the best students.

369 - Парень ['paren'] - A fellow, a guy; a boyfriend

В общем, он хороший **парень**, но очень просто выходит из себя.
He's a good **fellow** in general but he loses his temper easily.

370 - Кровь ['krov'] - *Blood*

Полиция пытается выяснить, чья это **кровь**.
The police are trying to find out whose **blood** it is.

371 - Двадцать ['dvatsat'] - *Twenty*

Мы приехали на вокзал за **двадцать** минут до отъезда.
We arrived at the railway station **twenty** minutes before the departure.

372 - Солнце ['sontse] - *The sun*

Солнце всходит на востоке.
The sun rises in the East.

373 - Неделя [n'e'delja] - *A week*

Мне нужна **неделя**, чтобы закончить эксперимент.
I need a **week** to finish the experiment.

374 - Послать [pas'lat'] - *To send*

Мы должны срочно **послать** за врачом!
We must **send** for the doctor urgently!

375 - Находиться [naha'ditsa] - *To be located*

Я уверен, что этот ресторан просто не может **находиться** так далеко.
I'm sure this restaurant just can't **be located** so far.

376 - Ребята [r'e'bjata] - Guys, young men (often used as vocative)

Ребята, пошли на каток!
Guys, let's go to the skating rink!

377 - Поставить [pas'tavit'] - *To put, to place (perfective)*

Где я могу **поставить** свои вещи?
Where can I **put** my things?

378 - Встать [vstat'] - *To stand up*

Он попытался **встать**, но у него кружилась голова.
He tried to **stand up** but he was dizzy.

379 - Например [napri'mer] - *For example*

Моя дочь не ест многие продукты, **например**, рыбу.
My daughter doesn't eat many foods, fish, **for example**.

380 - Шаг [shag] - *Step*

Это решение – очень серьёзный **шаг**.
This decision is a very serious **step**.

381 - Мужчина [muzh'china] - *A man*

Мой отец – замечательный **мужчина**.
My father is a remarkable **man**.

382 - Равно [rav'no] - In combination with 'всё' - In any case, It's all the same

Зачем мне волноваться? **Всё равно** это не моя проблема.
Why should I worry? **In any case**, it's not my problem.

383 - Нос [nos] - *A nose*

Сильный удар сломал ему **нос**.
A hard blow broke his **nose**.

384 - Мало ['malə] - *Little, few*

Для этой должности у вас слишком **мало** опыта.
You have too **little** experience for this position.

385 - Внимание [vni'manie] - *Attention*

Иногда **внимание** лучше любых подарков.
Sometimes **attention** is better than any present.

386 - Капитан [kapi'tan] - *A captain*

Капитан корабля был человеком с отличным чувством юмора.
The **captain** of the ship was a man with an excellent sense of humor.

387 - Ухо ['uhə] - *An ear*

Моя собака глухая на одно **ухо**.
My dog is deaf in one **ear**.

388 - Туда [tu'da] - *There*

В прошлом году я был в Париже и планирую вернуться **туда**.
Last year I was in Paris and I am planning to return **there**.

389 - Сюда [sju'da] - *Here, this way*

Как ты попал **сюда**?
How did you get **here**?

390 - Играть [ig'rat'] - *To play*

Я научился **играть** на скрипке, когда мне было двенадцать.
I learned **to play** the violin when I was twelve.

391 - Следовать ['sledavat'] - *To follow, to go after*

Я не хочу **следовать** этим правилам.
I don't want **to follow** these rules.

392 - Рассказать [raska'zat'] - *To tell (perfective)*

Дети всегда просят меня **рассказать** им сказку перед сном.
Children always ask me **to tell** them a fairy tale before bedtime.

393 - Великий [ve'likij] - *Great, outstanding*

Пушкин – **великий** русский поэт.
Pushkin is a **great** Russian poet.

394 - Действительно [dejst'vitelnə] - *Really, actually*

Я **действительно** ничего не знаю об аварии.
I **really** don't know anything about the accident.

395 - Слишком ['slishkəm] - *Too*

Современные дети **слишком** много времени проводят за компьютером.
Today's kids spend **too** much time on the computer.

396 - Тяжелый [tja'zhjelyj] - *Heavy; difficult, hard*

Я не могу сама нести этот чемодан – он очень **тяжёлый**.
I can't carry this suitcase myself – it's very **heavy**.

397 - Спать ['spat'] - *To sleep*

Она не может **спать** с включённым светом.
She can't **sleep** with the lights on.

398 - Оставить [as'tavit'] - *To leave; to abandon*

Как ты мог **оставить** паспорт дома?
How could you **leave** your passport at home?

399 - Войти [vaj'ti] - *To enter, to come in*

Я не смог **войти** в комнату – дверь была закрыта.
I couldn't **enter** the room – the door was closed.

400 - Длинный ['dlinnyj] - *Long*

Я люблю этот старый **длинный** шарф.
I love this old **long** scarf.

401 - Чувство ['tchustvə] - *A feeling*

Зависть – это плохое чувство.
Envy is a bad feeling.

402 - Молчать [mal'chat'] - *To keep silent*

Он попросил меня **молчать** о нашей ссоре.
He asked me **to keep silent** about our argument.

403 - Рассказывать [ras'kazyvat'] - *To tell*

Мой дедушка умел **рассказывать** интересные истории.
My grandfather could **tell** interesting stories.

404 - Отвечать [atve'tchat'] - *To answer, to reply*

Могу я не **отвечать** на этот вопрос?
May I not **answer** this question?

405 - Становиться [stana'vitsa] - *To become; to stand*

Вставать так поздно не должно **становиться** твоей привычкой.
Getting up so late shouldn't **become** your habit.

406 - Остановиться [astana'vitsa] - *To stop*

Мальчик понимал, что нельзя так сильно смеяться, но он просто не мог **остановиться**.
The boy realized he shouldn't laugh so much, but he just couldn't **stop**.

407 - Берег ['bereg] - *A bank, a shore*

Берег реки был покрыт густым кустарником.
The **bank** of the river was covered with thick bushes.

408 - Семья [sem'ja] - *A family*

Моя **семья** всегда меня поддерживает.
My **family** always supports me.

409 - Искать [is'kat'] - *To look for*

Он начал **искать** работу два месяца назад.
He started **to look for** work two months ago.

410 - Генерал [gene'ral] - *A general*

Мой дядя военный, он уже **генерал**.
My uncle is a military man, he's a **general** already.

411 - Момент [ma'ment] - *A moment*

Это уникальный **момент** в истории государства.
It's a unique **moment** in the history of the state.

412 - Десять ['desjat] - *Ten*

Мне нужно **десять** метров шёлка.
I need **ten** meters of silk.

413 - Начать [na'chat'] - *To start, to begin (perfective)*

Я даже не знаю, с чего **начать**.
I don't even know what **to start** with.

414 - Следующий ['sledujuschij] - *Next, following*

Каков наш **следующий** шаг?
What's our **next** step?

415 - Личный ['lichnyj] - *Personal*

У этого бизнесмена есть **личный** самолёт.
This businessman has a **personal** plane.

416 - Труд [trud] - *Labor, work*

Тяжёлый **труд** испортил его здоровье.
Hard **labor** spoiled his health.

417 - Верить ['verit'] - *To believe*

Не следует **верить** всему, что говорят по телевизору.
One shouldn't **believe** everything they say on TV.

418 - Группа ['grupa] - *A group*

Первая **группа** участников оказалась более талантливой.
The first **group** of the participants turned out to be more talented.

419 - Немного [nem'nogə] - *A little, some*

Я могу **немного** говорить по-русски.

I can speak Russian **a little**.

420 - Впрочем ['vprotchem] - *However*

Впрочем, я не против этого предложения.

However, I'm not against this proposal.

421 - Видно ['vidnə] - Looks like, evidently (colloquial)

Видно, ты забыл о своём обещании.

Looks like you forgot about your promise.

422 - Являться [jav'ljatsa] - To be (only imperfective); to turn up

Такое поведение не может **являться** нормой.

Such behavior can't **be** the norm.

423 - Муж [muzh] - *A husband*

Её **муж** – моряк.

Her **husband** is a sailor.

424 - Разве ['razve] - Really (mostly to express surprise)

Разве он уже потратил все деньги?

Has he **really** spent all the money already?

425 - Движение [dvi'zhenije] - *Movement, motion*

В балете каждое **движение** имеет значение.

Every **movement** matters in ballet.

426 - Порядок [po'rjadək] - *Order; sequence*

Пора привести дом в **порядок**.

It's time to put the house in **order**.

427 - Ответ [at'vet] - *Answer, reply*

Её **ответ** удивил всех.

Her **answer** surprised everyone.

428 - Тихо [ti'ho] - *Quietly*

У меня болит горло, поэтому я говорю так **тихо**.

I have a sore throat, that's why I talk so **quietly**.

429 - Знакомый [zna'komyj] - *An acquaintance, a friend; familiar*

Мне помог мой **знакомый** с работы.

My **acquaintance** from work helped me.

430 - Газета [ga'zeta] - *A newspaper*

Каждая **газета** в стране писала об этом.

Every **newspaper** in the country wrote about it.

431 - Помощь ['poməstch] - *Help*

Моя семья всегда рядом, когда мне нужна **помощь**.

My family is always there for me when I need **help**.

432 - Сильный ['sil'nyj] - *Strong*

Сильный ветер сдул его шляпу.

A **strong** wind blew off his hat.

433 - Скорый ['skoryj] - *Quick, rapid*

Его **скорый** отъезд удивил нас всех.

His **quick** departure surprised us all.

434 - Собака [sa'baka] - *A dog*

Эта **собака** – победитель многих конкурсов.
This **dog** is the winner of many competitions.

435 - Дерево ['derevə] - *A tree*

Мой дедушка посадил это **дерево**, когда был молодым.
My grandfather planted this **tree** when he was young.

436 - Снег [sneg] - *Snow*

Белый **снег** искрился на солнце.
White **snow** was sparkling in the sun.

437 - Сон [son] - *Sleep; dream*

Здоровый **сон** – это главное условие его выздоровления.
Sound **sleep** is the main condition for his recovery.

438 - Смысл [smysl] - *Sense, meaning*

Я не совсем понимаю **смысл** этой пословицы.
I don't quite understand the **sense** of this proverb.

439 - Смочь [smoch'] - *To manage, to be able to (perfective, isn't used in the initial form, in the example below past 3d person singular masculine form is used)*

Наконец, спортсмен **смог** побить свой собственный рекорд.
At last, the athlete **managed** to beat his own record.

440 - Против ['protiv] - *Against*

Родители были **против** их отношений.
The parents were **against** their relationship.

441 - Бежать [be'zhat'] - *To run*

Ей пришлось **бежать**, чтобы успеть на автобус.
She had **to run** to catch the bus.

442 - Двор [dvor] - *A yard*

Мы украсили **двор** к празднику.
We decorated the **yard** for the holiday.

443 - Форма ['forma] - *A shape, a form*

У этого предмета была странная **форма**.
That object had a strange **shape**.

444 - Простой [pras'toj] - *Simple*

Это очень **простой** вопрос, задай мне другой.
It's a very **simple** question, ask me another one.

445 - Приехать [pri'jehat'] - **To arrive to, to come (perfective)**

Не злись на него – он не мог **приехать** раньше.
Don't be angry with him – he couldn't **arrive** earlier.

446 - Иной [i'noj] - **Different, other, another (more literary style)**

Он так не похож на брата, у него совсем **иной** характер.
He's so much unlike his brother, he has a completely **different** character.

447 - Кричать [kri'tchat'] - *To cry, to shout, to scream*

Не нужно **кричать** – я прекрасно тебя слышу.
There's no need to **cry** – I can hear you perfectly well.

448 - Возможность [vaz'mozhnəst'] - *An opportunity; a possibility*

Она упустила **возможность** получить новую работу.
She missed the **opportunity** to get a new job.

449 - Общество ['obstchestvə] - *A society; a community*

Общество не всегда продвигает правильные ценности.
The **society** doesn't always promote the right values.

450 - Зелёный [ze'l'onyj] - *Green*

Считается, что **зелёный** цвет помогает успокоиться.
It's considered that **green** color helps to calm down.

451 - Грудь [grud'] - *Chest; breast*

Неожиданный выстрел в **грудь** убил полицейского.
A sudden shot in the **chest** killed the policeman.

452 - Угол ['ugəl] - *A corner; an angle*

Угол здания был неровным.
The **corner** of the building was uneven.

453 - Открыть [ot'kryt'] - *To open; to discover*

Преступник не смог **открыть** сейф.
The criminal didn't manage **to open** the safe.

454 - Происходить [praisha'dit'] - *To take place; to happen*

Подобное не должно **происходить** в нашей стране.
Such things shouldn't **happen** in our country.

455 - Ладно ['ladnə] - *All right, okay*

Ладно, я помогу тебе с докладом, но это в последний раз.

All right, I'll help you with the report, but it's the last time.

456 - Оранжевый [a'ranzhevyj] - *Orange (color)*

Сними этот **оранжевый** костюм. Ты в нём выглядишь как клоун.

Take this **orange** suit off. You look like a clown in it.

457 - Век [vek] - *Century, age*

Двадцать первый **век** – это эпоха информационных технологий.

The twenty first **century** is the age of information technology.

458 - Карман [kar'man] - *A pocket*

Карман джинсов не самое надёжное место для ключей.

A jeans **pocket** is not the most reliable place for keys.

459 - Ехать ['jehat'] - *To go (by horse or vehicle), to ride, to drive*

Вы сейчас же должны **ехать** в больницу.

You must **go** to hospital at once.

460 - Немец ['nemets] - *German, a German man*

Никто не знает, что он **немец**.

Nobody knows he's **German**.

461 - Наверное [na'vernəje] - *Probably, likely*

Он, **наверное**, самый известный русский актёр.

He's **probably** the most famous Russian actor.

462 - Губа [gu'ba] - *A lip*

Верхняя **губа** ребенка распухла от укуса пчелы.

The child's upper **lip** is swollen from a bee sting.

463 - Дядя ['djadja] - **An uncle; a man (colloquial)**

Мой **дядя** профессиональный фотограф.

My **uncle** is a professional photographer.

464 - Приходить [priha'dit'] - *To come; to arrive at*

Я обещаю **приходить** каждый день и навещать тебя в больнице.

I promise **to come** every day and visit you in the hospital.

465 - Часто ['tchastə] - *Often*

Мы с женой **часто** вспоминаем день нашего знакомства.

My wife and I **often** recollect the day we met.

466 - Домой [da'moj] - **Home (direction, where to)**

Темнеет, мне пора **домой**.

It's getting dark, it's time for me to go **home**.

467 - Огонь [a'gon'] - *Fire*

Твои слова только добавляют масла в **огонь**.

Your words are only adding fuel to the **fire**.

468 - Писатель [pi'satel'] - *A writer*

Кто твой любимый американский **писатель**?

Who's your favorite American **writer**?

469 - Армия ['armija] - *The army*

Армия должна защищать население страны.

The army must protect the population of the country.

470 - Состояние [sasta'janije] - *State, condition; fortune*

Состояние этой машины оставляет желать лучшего.

The **state** of this car leaves much to be desired.

471 - Зуб [zub] - *A tooth*

Стоматолог аккуратно удалил гнилой **зуб**.

The dentist carefully removed the decayed **tooth**.

472 - Очередь ['otchered'] - *A queue*

Перед Эрмитажем всегда большая **очередь**.

There's always a long **queue** in front of the Hermitage.

473 - Кой [koj] - **In the expression 'на кой чёрт' - 'Why the hell?'**

На кой чёрт ты купил все эти вещи?

Why the hell have you bought all these things?

474 - Подняться [pad'n'atsatsa] - *To rise, to go up, to get up*

Как цены могли **подняться** так быстро?

How could the prices **rise** so quickly?

475 - Камень ['kamen'] - *A stone; a rock*

Вчера из музея был украден драгоценный **камень**.

Yesterday a precious **stone** was stolen from the museum.

476 - Гость [gost'] - *A guest*

Расслабься и получай удовольствие – ты наш **гость**.

Relax and enjoy – you're our **guest**.

477 - Показаться [paka'zatsa] - *To seem, to appear*

Её поведение может **показаться** странным, но ты привыкнешь к этому.
Her behavior may **seem** strange, but you'll get used to it.

478 - Ветер ['veter] - *Wind*

Вчерашний сильный **ветер** нанес ущерб многим домам.
Yesterday's strong **wind** did harm to many houses.

479 - Собираться [sabi'ratsa] - *To gather; to be about to*

Мы любим **собираться** у родителей по праздникам.
We like to **gather** at our parents' on holidays.

480 - Попасть [pa'past'] - *To get to; to hit (a target) (perfective)*

Как ты смог **попасть** сюда без билета?
How did you manage to **get** here without a ticket?

481 - Принять [pri'njat'] - *To take; to admit (perfective)*

Мы должны **принять** срочные меры, пока ещё не поздно.
We must **take** urgent measures before it's too late.

482 - Сначала [sna'tchala] - *At first*

Сначала я не был уверен в своём решении.
At first I wasn't sure about my decision.

483 - Либо ['libə] - *Either ... or, or*

Он **либо** действительно ничего не знает, **либо** притворяется.
He **either** really doesn't know anything **or** is pretending.

484 - Поехать [pa'jehat'] - To go (by horse or vehicle), to ride, to drive (perfective)

Извини, я не смогу **поехать** с тобой за город.
Sorry, I won't be able **to go** to the country with you.

485 - Услышать [us'lyshat'] - *To hear (perfective)*

Я бы так хотела **услышать** её пение!
I would so much like **to hear** her singing!

486 - Уметь [u'met'] - To be able to, to know how to

Ты должен **уметь** прощать, если хочешь сохранить свою семью.
You should **be able to** forgive if you want to keep your family.

487 - Случиться [slu'tchitsa] - *To happen, to occur*

Не волнуйся так сильно! Что могло **случиться**?
Don't worry so much! What could have **happened**?

488 - Странный ['strannyj] - *Strange*

Что это за **странный** запах?
What kind of **strange** smell is it?

489 - Единственный [je'dinstvennyj] - *Only, sole*

Он **единственный** ребёнок в семье.
He's an **only** child in the family.

490 - Рота ['rota] - *Company (military)*

Одна **рота** не может сражаться против целой армии.
One **company** can't fight against the whole army.

491 - Закон [za'kon] - *Law*

Закон один для всех.
The **law** is the same for everyone.

492 - Короткий [ka'rotkij] - *Short*

Этот курс **короткий**, но очень полезный.
This course is **short** but very useful.

493 - Море ['more] - *Sea*

Мёртвое **море** – самое солёное в мире.
The Dead **Sea** is the saltiest in the world.

494 - Добрый ['dobryj] - *Kind*

Мой друг очень **добрый** и всегда готов помочь.
My friend is very **kind** and is always ready to help.

495 - Тёмный ['tjemnyj] - *Dark*

Большинство детей не любят **тёмный** шоколад.
Most children don't like **dark** chocolate.

496 - Гора [ga'ra] - *A mountain*

Эта **гора** выглядит очень живописно.
This **mountain** looks very picturesque.

497 - Врач [vratch] - *A doctor, a physician*

Наш семейный **врач** – очень ответственный человек.
Our family **doctor** is a very responsible man.

498 - Край [kraj] - *An edge; a land*

Край ножа был очень острым.
The **edge** of the knife was very sharp.

499 - Стараться [sta'ratsa] - *To try, to attempt*

Я буду **стараться** изо всех сил.
I'll **try** my best.

500 - Лучший ['lutchij] - *The best*

Он **лучший** игрок в команде.

He's **the best** player in the team.

501 - Река [re'ka] - *A river*

Эта **река** опасная: она глубокая и течение очень сильное.

This **river** is dangerous: it's deep and the current is very strong.

502 - Военный [va'jennyj] - *A military man; military*

Мой папа **военный**, поэтому мы часто переезжаем.

My father is **a military man;** that is why we often move around.

503 - Мера ['mera] - *A measure, a degree*

Эта **мера** очень радикальная, но это единственный выход.

This **measure** is very radical, but it's the only way out.

504 - Страшный ['strashnyj] - *Terrible, scary*

Страшный ураган разрушил всю деревню.

A **terrible** hurricane destroyed the whole village.

505 - Вполне [vpal'ne] - *Quite, fully*

Я не **вполне** понимаю, что вы имеете в виду.

I don't **quite** understand what you mean.

506 - Звать ['zvat'] - *To call; to invite*

Я не люблю **звать** людей по фамилии.

I don't like **to call** people by their last name.

507 - Произойти [praizaj'ty] - *To take place, to happen (perfective)*

Такое событие могло **произойти** только в Европе.

Such an event could **take place** only in Europe.

508 - Вперёд [vpe'rjed] - *Forward; in advance*

Мы должны двигаться **вперёд** и верить в наши идеалы.
We must move **forward** and believe in our values.

509 - Медленный ['medlennyj] - *Slow*

Этот поезд такой **медленный**! Когда мы прибудем на нашу станцию?
This train is so **slow**! When will we arrive at our station?

510 - Возле ['vozle] - *Beside, by, near*

Возле моей кровати стоит небольшая книжная полка.
There's a little book shelf standing **beside** my bed.

511 - Никак [ni'kak] - *In no way, by no means*

Эту картину **никак** нельзя назвать шедевром.
This painting is **in no way** a masterpiece.

512 - Заниматься [zani'matsa] - *To engage in; to study*

Он хочет **заниматься** научными исследованиями.
He wants **to engage in** scientific research.

513 - Действие ['dejstvije] - *An action*

Некоторые родители контролируют каждое **действие** своего ребёнка.
Some parents control every **action** their child takes.

514 - Довольно [da'volnə] - *Quite; enough*

Он **довольно** сдержанный человек.
He's **quite** a reserved man.

71

515 - Вещь [vestch] - *A thing; a matter*

Как ты мог взять эту **вещь** без разрешения?

How could you take this **thing** without asking?

516 - Необходимый [neobho'dimyj] - *Necessary, required*

У вас есть **необходимый** инструмент, чтобы закончить работу?

Do you have the **necessary** tool to finish the work?

517 - Ход [hod] - *A move; course*

Это был очень хорошо продуманный **ход**.

That was a very well-thought **move**.

518 - Боль [bol'] - *Pain*

Ужасная **боль** не давала ей спать по ночам.

A terrible **pain** prevented her from sleeping at night.

519 - Судьба [syd''ba] - *Destiny, fate*

Ты уверена, что этот мужчина – твоя **судьба**?

Are you sure this man is your **destiny**?

520 - Причина [pri'china] - *A reason, a cause*

Какова **причина** вашей ссоры?

What's the **reason** for your quarrel?

521 - Положить [pala'zhit'] - *To put, to lay down (perfective)*

Не забудь **положить** мороженое в холодильник.

Don't forget **to put** the ice-cream into the fridge.

522 - Едва [jed'va] - *Barely*

У него очень плохое произношение, поэтому я **едва** понимаю, что он говорит.

He's got a very bad pronunciation, that's why I **barely** understand what he says.

523 - Черта [tcher'ta] - *A feature, a trait; a line*

Интуитивный интерфейс – это лучшая **черта** этого приложения.

Intuitive interface is the best **feature** of this application.

524 - Девочка ['devachka] - *A girl*

Девочка была напугана и не могла перестать плакать.

The **girl** was scared and couldn't stop crying.

525 - Лёгкий ['ljehkij] - *Light, lightweight; easy*

Прими **лёгкий** душ и расслабься.

Take a **light** shower and relax.

526 - Волос ['voləs] - *A hair*

Официант, у меня **волос** в тарелке!

Waiter, there's a **hair** in my plate!

527 - Купить [ku'pit'] - *To buy, to purchase*

Мы не можем позволить себе **купить** эту машину.

We can't afford **to buy** this car.

528 - Номер ['nomer] - *A number*

Я опять потерял **номер** твоего телефона.

I lost your phone **number** again.

529 - Основной [asnav'noj] - *Major, basic*

Мы делаем **основной** упор на развитие экономики.
We place **major** emphasis on the development of the economy.

530 - Широкий [shi'rokij] - *Wide, broad*

Мы предлагаем **широкий** выбор товаров.
We offer a **wide** choice of goods.

531 - Умереть [ume'ret'] - *To die (perfective)*

Я не готов **умереть** за политические идеи.
I'm not ready **to die** for political ideas.

532 - Плохо ['plohə] - *Bad, badly*

Ты **плохо** выглядишь. Что случилось?
You look **bad**. What's happened?

533 - Глава [gla'va] - *A head (someone in charge, not part of the body); a chapter*

Глава государства должен уметь брать на себя ответственность.
The **head** of state must be able to take on responsibility.

534 - Красивый [kra'sivyj] - *Beautiful*

Красивый закат окрасил море в красный цвет.
A **beautiful** sunset painted the sea in red color.

535 - Серый ['seryj] - *Grey, gray*

Этот **серый** плащ делает тебя старше. Сними его!
This **grey** raincoat makes you look older. Take it off!

536 - Пить ['pit'] - *To drink*

Я не могу **пить** такой крепкий кофе.
I can't **drink** such strong coffee.

537 - Командир [kaman'dir] - A commander, a commanding officer (military)

Командир приказал солдатам отступать.

The **commander** ordered the soldiers to retreat.

538 - Обычно [a'bychnə] - *Usually*

Обычно отчёт занимает у меня больше времени.

The report **usually** takes me more time.

539 - Партия ['partija] - A party (political group); a batch

Демократическая **партия** проиграла на прошлых выборах.

The democratic **party** lost at the last elections.

540 - Проблема [prab'lema] - *A problem*

Поверь мне, порванное платье – это не **проблема**.

Believe me, a torn dress is not a **problem**.

541 - Страх [strah] - *A fear*

Страх потерять работу сделал её очень нервной.

The **fear** of losing her job made her very nervous.

542 - Проходить [praha'dit'] - *To pass, to pass by*

Дорога к дому будет **проходить** через зелёную лужайку.

The path to the house will **pass** through a green lawn.

543 - Ясно ['jasnə] - *Clearly, distinctly*

В инструкции **ясно** говорится, что прибор нельзя использовать в воде.

The instruction **clearly** states that the device can't be used in water.

544 - Снять [snjat'] - To take off; to take down (perfective)

Ребёнок попросил маму **снять** ему обувь.

The child asked his mom to **take off** his shoes.

545 - Бумага [bu'maga] - *Paper*

Эта **бумага** сделана из переработанной древесины.

This **paper** is made of recycled wood.

546 - Герой [ge'roj] - *A hero; a character*

Мой дедушка – **герой** войны, и мы им очень гордимся.

My grandfather is **a** war **hero** and we're very proud of him.

547 - Пара ['para] - *A couple, a pair*

У меня есть **пара** идей насчёт новой гостиницы.

I have **a couple** ideas about the new hotel.

548 - Государство [gasu'darstvə] - *A state (government)*

Любое **государство** должно защищать интересы своих граждан.

Any **state** must protect the interests of its citizens.

549 - Деревня [de'rjevnja] - *A village; the countryside*

Раньше эта **деревня** была самой большой в районе.

This **village** used to be the largest in the area.

550 - Речь ['retch] - *A speech, a language*

Его **речь** полна грубых слов и грамматических ошибок.

His **speech** is full of rude words and grammar mistakes.

551 - Начаться [na'tchatsa] - To begin, to start (perfective)

Пьеса должна была **начаться** пятнадцать минут назад.

The play should have **begun** fifteen minutes ago.

552 - Средство ['sredstvə] - *A means*

Мобильный телефон – это самое популярное **средство** связи сегодня.

A mobile phone is the most popular **means** of communication today.

553 - Положение [pala'zhenije] - *A situation; a location*

Не расстраивайся! Наше **положение** ещё не худшее.

Don't get upset! Our **situation** is not yet the worst one.

554 - Связь [svjaz'] - *A link, a connection*

Какова **связь** между этими двумя ограблениями?

What's the **link** between these two robberies?

555 - Скоро ['skorə] - *Soon*

Скоро мы узнаем результаты экзамена.

We'll know the exam results **soon**.

556 - Небольшой [nebal'shoj] - *Small, little*

За домом есть **небольшой** сад со скамейкой и качелями.

There's a **small** garden behind the house with a bench and a swing.

557 - Представлять [predstav'ljat'] - *To imagine; to represent; to introduce*

Мне не нужно **представлять**, как выглядит это здание – я его видел.

I don't need to **imagine** what this building looks like – I've seen it.

558 - Завтра ['zavtra] - *Tomorrow*

Я не думаю, что погода **завтра** изменится к лучшему.
I don't think the weather will change for the better **tomorrow**.

559 - Объяснить [abjas'nit'] - *To explain (perfective)*

Невозможно **объяснить**, что такое любовь.
It's impossible **to explain** what love is.

560 - Пустой [pus'toj] - *Empty*

Пустой дом выглядел холодным и чужим.
The **empty** house looked cold and alien.

561 - Произнести [praiznes'ti] - To pronounce, to articulate (perfective)

Я не могу **произнести** некоторые русские слова.
I can't **pronounce** some Russian words.

562 - Человеческий [thela'vetcheskij] - *Human (adj); humane*

Человеческий организм – это сложный механизм.
A human **organism** is a complicated mechanism.

563 - Нравиться ['nravitsa] - To like (the person who likes takes the dative case)

Как тебе могут **нравиться** эти картины?
How can you **like** these paintings?

564 - Однажды [ad'nazhdy] - One day, once, once upon a time

Однажды ты встретишь свою судьбу и будешь счастлива.
One day you'll meet your destiny and you will be happy.

565 - Мимо ['mimə] - *Past (preposition)*

Он прошёл **мимо** нас, как будто никогда не знал нас.
He went **past** us as if he never used to know us.

566 - Иначе [i'natche] - *Otherwise, or else*

Тебе следует уделять больше внимания учёбе, **иначе** ты не сдашь экзамен.
You should pay more attention to the studies, **otherwise** you won't pass the exam.

567- Существовать [sustchestva'vat'] - *To exist*

Жизнь на Земле не может **существовать** без воды.
Life on Earth can't **exist** without water.

568 - Класс [klas] - **A class; a classroom; a grade**

Дети, ваш **класс** самый шумный в школе!
Kids, your **class** is the noisiest in the school!

569 - Удаться [u'datsa] - **To turn out well, to be a success**

Это представление просто не могло **удаться** – оно было ужасным!
That performance just couldn't **turn out well** – it was horrible!

570 - Толстый ['tolstyj] - *Fat; thick*

Я и подумать не мог, что он был такой **толстый**.
I couldn't even think he used to be so **fat**.

571 - Цель [tsel'] - **A goal, an aim; a purpose**

Наша **цель** собрать как можно больше информации.
Our **goal** is to gather as much information as possible.

572 - Сквозь [skvoz'] - *Through*

Это окно настолько грязное, что я ничего **сквозь** него не вижу.
The window is so dirty that I don't see anything **through** it.

573 - Прийтись [prij'tis'] - *To fall on (a date) (perfective)*

Фестиваль должен **прийтись** на те же даты.
The festival must **fall on** the same date.

574 - Чистый ['tchistyj] - *Clean; tidy*

Я вижу, ты убиралась дома – пол такой **чистый**.
I see you've tidied the house – the floor is so **clean**.

575 - Знать [znat'] - *To know*

Она была за границей и поэтому не могла **знать** о том, что случилось.
She was abroad, so she couldn't **know** about what had happened.

576 - Прежний ['prezhnij] - *Former, previous*

Наш **прежний** учитель был более дружелюбный.
Our **former** teacher was more friendly.

577 - Профессор [pra'fesər] - *A professor*

Профессор всегда был требователен к своим студентам.
The **professor** was always demanding to his students.

578 - Господин [gəspa'din] - *A gentleman, mister*

Этот уважаемый **господин** много жертвует на благотворительность.
This respected **gentleman** donates a lot to charity.

579 - Счастье ['shastje] - *Happiness*

Каждый понимает **счастье** по-разному.
Every person understands **happiness** in a different way.

580 - Худой [hu'doj] - *Thin, skinny*

Мальчик должен есть больше – он слишком **худой**.
The boy should eat more – he's too **thin**.

581 - Дух [duh] - *A spirit; a ghost*

Ничто не смогло сломить его сильный **дух**.
Nothing could break his strong **spirit**.

582 - План [plan] - *A plan*

Он придумал безупречный **план**.
He came up with an impeccable **plan**.

583 - Чужой [tchu'zhoj] - *Someone else's; alien*

Это **чужой** кошелёк, он просто похож на мой.
It's **someone else's** purse, it just resembles mine.

584 - Зал [zal] - *A hall; a living room*

Зал был украшен цветами и лентами.
The **hall** was decorated with flowers and ribbons.

585 - Представить [preds'tavit]' - *To imagine; to represent; to introduce (perfective)*

Я не могу **представить** свою жизнь без своих детей.
I can't **imagine** my life without my children.

586 - Особый [a'sobyj] - *Special, particular*

Я хочу подарить ей **особый** подарок.
I want to give her a **special** present.

587 - Директор [di'rectər] - *A manager, a director*

Наш **директор** – очень хороший лидер.
Our **manager** is a very good leader.

588 - Бывший ['byvshyj] - *Ex-, former*

Бывший президент все ещё активно участвует в жизни страны.
The **ex-**president still actively participates in the life of the country.

589 - Память ['pamjat'] - *Memory*

Учёные говорят, что **память** можно тренировать.
Scientists say that **memory** can be trained.

590 - Близкий ['blizkij] - *Close*

Он мой **близкий** друг, и я могу доверить ему что угодно.
He's my **close** friend and I can trust him with anything.

591 - Сей [sej] - *This (archaic, literary, has a humorous connotation if used in everyday speech)*

Ну, что нам говорит **сей** документ?
Well, what does **this** document tell us?

592 - Результат [rezul'tat] - *A result*

Деньги не проблема – для меня важен **результат**.
Money is not a problem; what matters to me is the **result**.

593 - Больной [bal'noj] - *Sick, ill; a patient*

Больной ребёнок не спал всю ночь.
The **sick** child didn't sleep the whole night.

594 - Данный ['dannyj] - *Given, present*

Данный аргумент помог мне доказать, что я прав.
The **given** argument helped me to prove that I was right.

595 - Кстати [ks'tati] - *By the way*

Кстати, не забудь выгулять собаку.
By the way, don't forget to walk the dog.

596 - Назвать [naz'vat'] - *To name, to call (perfective)*

Они ещё не решили, как **назвать** новую улицу.
They have not yet decided what **to name** the new street.

597 - След [sled] - *Track; a footprint*

Собака потеряла **след** волка.
The dog lost the wolf's **track**.

598 - Улыбаться [uly'batsa] - *To smile*

Моя сестра умеет **улыбаться**, как никто другой.
My sister can **smile** like nobody else.

599 - Бутылка [bu'tylka] - *A bottle*

Стеклянная **бутылка** упала и разбилась на сотни кусочков.
A glass **bottle** fell down and broke into hundreds of pieces.

600 - Трудно ['trudnə] - *It is difficult, hard*

Трудно совмещать работу и учёбу.
It is difficult to combine work and studies.

601 - Условие [us'lovije] - *A condition*

У меня только одно **условие** – свободный график.
I have only one **condition** – a flexible schedule.

602 - Прежде ['prezhde] - *Before, previously*

После отдыха я чувствую себя гораздо лучше, чем **прежде**.
After the rest I feel much better than **before**.

603 - Ум [um] - *Mind, intellect*

Кроссворды стимулируют **ум**.
Crossword puzzles stimulate the **mind**.

604 - Улыбнуться [ulyb'nutsa] - *To smile (perfective)*

Фотограф попросил нас **улыбнуться**.
The photographer asked us **to smile**.

605 - Процесс [pra'tses] - *A process*

Процесс приготовления этого блюда очень долгий.
The **process** of preparation of this dish is very long.

606 - Картина [kar'tina] - *A picture, a painting*

Эта **картина** на стене стоит состояние.
This **picture** on the wall costs a fortune.

607 - Вместо ['vmestə] - *Instead of*

Вместо того, чтобы помочь мне, ты даёшь мне бесполезные советы.
Instead of helping me you are giving me useless advice.

608 - Старший ['starshij] - *Elder, older, senior*

Её **старший** брат часто попадает в неприятности.
Her **elder** brother often gets into trouble.

609 - Центр [tsentr] - *Center, centre*

Мы пошли в **центр** города, чтобы увидеть знаменитый собор.
We went to the **center** of the city to see the famous cathedral.

610 - Подобный [pa'dobnyj] - *Such, similar*

Подобный подход не поможет решить проблему.
Such an approach won't help to solve the problem.

611 - Возможный [voz'mozhnyj] - *Possible*

Возможный союз двух государств может принести много пользы.

The **possible** unity of the two states may do a lot of good.

612 - Около ['okələ] - *Near, around; about*

Твой бумажник на столе, **около** книг.

Your wallet is on the table, **near** the books.

613 - Смеяться [sme'jatsa] - *To laugh*

Перестань шутить – я больше не могу **смеяться**.

Stop joking – I can't **laugh** anymore.

614 - Сто [sto] - *A hundred*

Я **сто** раз говорила тебе не трогать мои украшения!

I told you **a hundred** times not to touch my jewelry!

615 - Будущее ['budustcheje] - *Future*

Говорят, некоторые люди могут предсказывать **будущее**.

They say some people can tell the **future**.

616 - Хватать [hva'tat'] - To be enough (Impersonal, not used in the initial form)

Тебе **хватит** этой суммы на неделю?

Will this sum **be enough** for you for a week?

617 - Число [tchis'lo] - *A number; a date*

Ты веришь в то, что семь – это счастливое **число**?

Do you believe that seven is a lucky **number**?

618 - Всякое ['fs'akaje] - *Things, stuff*

Они будут говорить тебе **всякое** про меня, но не верь им.

They're going to tell you **things** about me but don't believe them.

619 - Рубль [rubl'] - *A ruble*

Рубль – это российская валюта.
The ruble is the Russian currency.

620 - Почувствовать [pat'chustvəvat'] - *To feel (perfective)*

Это нельзя объяснить, ты должен сам **почувствовать** это.
This can't be explained, you must **feel** it yourself.

621 - Принести [prines'ti] - *To bring (perfective)*

Не могла бы ты **принести** мне печенье из кухни?
Could you **bring** me some cookies from the kitchen?

622 - Вера ['vera] - *A faith, belief; religion*

Её **вера** в Бога очень сильна.
Her **faith** in God is very strong.

623 - Вовсе ['vovse] - *At all*

Можешь оставить это платье, я не ношу его **вовсе**.
You can keep this dress, I don't wear it **at all**.

624 - Удар [u'dar] - *A blow, a strike*

Мощный **удар** противника нокаутировал боксёра.
The opponent's powerful **blow** knocked the boxer out.

625 - Телефон [tele'fon] - *A telephone*

По моему мнению, **телефон** – самое полезное изобретение.
In my opinion, the **phone** is the most useful invention.

626 - Колено [ka'lenə] - *A knee*

Моё **колено** болит так сильно, что я не могу ходить.
My **knee** hurts so much that I can't walk.

627 - Согласиться [sagla'sitsa] - *To agree (perfective)*

При всём уважении, я не могу **согласиться** с вами.
With due respect I can't **agree** with you.

628 - Коридор [kari'dor] - *A corridor*

Длинный, узкий **коридор** больницы был пуст.
The long, narrow **corridor** of the hospital was empty.

629 - Мужик [mu'zhik] - A man (colloquial implying a male with lots of masculinity, able to take on responsibility and do manly deeds)

Ты можешь положиться на него – он настоящий **мужик**.
You can rely on him – he's a real **man**.

630 - Правый ['pravyj] - *Right, right-hand*

Его **правый** глаз видит лучше, чем левый.
His **right** eye can see better than the left one.

631 - Автор ['avtər] - *Author*

Он **автор** многих бестселлеров.
He's the **author** of many bestsellers.

632 - Холодный [ha'lodnyj] - *Cold*

Не пей сок: он слишком **холодный**.
Don't drink the juice: it's too **cold**.

633 - Хватить [hva'tit'] - To be enough (perfective, unlike 'хватать' can be used in the initial form)

Этого времени должно **хватить**, чтобы успеть в срок.
This amount of time should **be enough** to meet a deadline.

634 - Многие ['mnogije] - *Many (people)*

Многие говорят, что жизнь стала тяжелее.
Many are saying that life has become harder.

635 - Встреча ['vstrecha] - *A meeting, an encounter*

Встреча с этим человеком изменила всю его жизнь.
The **meeting** with this man changed all his life.

636 - Кабинет [kabi'net] - *An office, a private office*

Кабинет начальника на втором этаже.
The manager's **office** is on the second floor.

637 - Документ [daku'ment] - *A document*

Мы рады, что наконец подписали этот **документ**.
We're happy that we've signed this **document** at last.

638 - Самолёт [sama'ljot] - *An airplane, a plane*

Самолёт срочно приземлился из-за плохой погоды.
The **airplane** landed urgently because of the bad weather.

639 - Вниз [vniz] - *Down, downwards*

Не смотри **вниз**, иначе упадёшь!
Don't look **down** or you'll fall!

640 - Принимать [prini'mat'] - *To take; to admit*

Ты должен **принимать** эти витамины два раза в день.
You should **take** these vitamins two times a day.

641 - Игра [ig'ra] - *A game*

Какая твоя любимая компьютерная **игра**?
What's your favorite computer **game**?

642 - Рассказ [ras'kaz] - A story, a narrative; a short story

Её **рассказ** о поездке оказался очень увлекательным.
Her **story** about the trip turned out to be very exciting.

643 - Хлеб [hleb] - *Bread*

Она на диете и не ест **хлеб**.
She's on a diet and doesn't eat any **bread**.

644 - Развитие [raz'vitije] - *Development*

Физическое **развитие** ребёнка зависит от правильного питания.
Physical **development** of a child depends on proper nutrition.

645 - Убить [u'bit'] - *To kill*

Я не уверена, что смогу **убить** живое существо.
I'm not sure I'll be able **to kill** a living being.

646 - Родной [rad'noj] - *Native; dear*

Мой **родной** город много значит для меня.
My **native** town means much to me.

647 - Открытый [atk'rytyj] - *Open; public*

Спасибо за **открытый** диалог.
Thank you for the **open** dialog.

648 - Менее ['meneje] - *Less*

Этот учебник **менее** сложный для начинающих.
This textbook is **less** difficult for beginners.

649 - Предложить [predla'zhit'] - To offer; to suggest; to propose (perfective)

Я могу **предложить** вам более доступный вариант.

I can **offer** you a more affordable option.

650 - Жёлтый ['zholtyj] - *Yellow*

В вазе стоит яркий **жёлтый** подсолнух.

There's a bright **yellow** sunflower in the vase.

651 - Приходится [pri'hoditsa] - *To have to (impersonal)*

Я живу за городом, поэтому мне **приходится** рано вставать, чтобы успеть на работу.

I live in the country, which is why I **have to** wake up early to be in time for work.

652 - Выпить ['vypit'] - To drink; to have a drink (perfective)

Кто мог **выпить** весь лимонад?

Who could **drink** all the lemonade?

653 - Крикнуть ['kriknut'] - To cry out, to scream (perfective)

Попробуй **крикнуть** громче, может, они не слышат тебя.

Try **to cry out** louder, maybe they don't hear you.

654 - Трубка ['trubka] - *A tube; a roll*

Там в ящике лежит металлическая **трубка**. Передай мне её, пожалуйста.

There's a metal **tube** there in the drawer. Pass it over to me, please.

655 - Враг [vrag] - *An enemy, a foe*

Лень – мой худший **враг**.

Laziness is my worst **enemy**.

656 - Показывать [pa'kazyvat'] - *To show*

Мы не хотим никому **показывать** ребёнка, пока не покрестим его.

We don't want **to show** the baby to anyone before we baptise him.

657 - Двое ['dvoje] - **Two (in a group together), two of**

Вы **двое**, идите за мной!

You **two**, follow me!

658 - Доктор ['doktər] - *A doctor (medical)*

Доктор настаивал на операции.

The **doctor** insisted on the surgery.

659 - Ладонь [la'don'] - *A palm (of the hand)*

Цыганка попросила показать ей мою правую **ладонь**.

The gypsy woman asked me to show her my right **palm**.

660 - Вызвать ['vyzvat'] - **To call, to send for (perfective)**

Мы должны сейчас же **вызвать** скорую.

We must **call** the ambulance at once.

661 - Спокойно [spa'kojnə] - *Calmly, quietly*

Пожалуйста, объясни всё **спокойно** и без крика.

Explain everything **calmly** and without screaming, please.

662 - Попросить [papra'sit'] - To ask for, to ask, to request (perfective)

Он пришёл, чтобы **попросить** о помощи.

He came to **ask for** help.

663 - Наука [na'uka] - *Science*

Есть очень много вещей, которые **наука** не может объяснить.

There're lots of things **science** can't explain.

664 - Лейтенант [lejte'nant] - *A lieutenant*

Молодой **лейтенант** мечтал о большой карьере.

The young **lieutenant** dreamed of a great career.

665 - Служба ['sluzhba] - *Service; employment*

Военная **служба** сделала его более организованным человеком.

Military **service** made him a better organized person.

666 - Оказываться [a'kazyvatsa] - *To find oneself; to turn out*

Никто не любит **оказываться** в неловких ситуациях.

Nobody likes **to find themselves** in awkward situations.

667 - Привести [prives'ti] - To bring (someone with); to lead to (perfective)

Можно мне **привести** с собой сестру на вечеринку?

May I **bring** my sister to the party with me?

668 - Сорок ['sorək] - *Forty*

Ему **сорок**, но он выглядит гораздо старше.

He's **forty** but he looks much older.

669 - Счёт [schot] - *An account; a bill*

Банковский **счёт** компании заблокирован.
The bank **account** of the company is blocked.

670 - Возвращаться [vazvra'stchatsa] - *To return, to come back*

Мы не хотим **возвращаться** в свою старую квартиру.
We don't want **to return** to our old flat.

671 - Золотой [zala'toj] - *Gold, golden*

Этот **золотой** медальон принадлежал моей бабушке.
This **gold** medallion used to belong to my grandmother.

672 - Местный ['mesnyj] - *Local*

Этот мужчина – **местный** гений.
This man is a **local** genius.

673 - Кухня ['kuhnja] - *A kitchen; cuisine*

Наша **кухня** просторная и светлая.
Our **kitchen** is spacious and light.

674 - Крупный ['krupnyj] - *Large, massive*

Мы получили **крупный** заказ, так что придётся много работать.
We got a **large** order, so we'll have to work a lot.

675 - Решение [re'shenije] - *A decision; a solution*

У вас есть два дня, чтобы принять **решение**.
You have two days to make a **decision**.

676 - Молодая [mala'daja] - Young (this form is used with feminine nouns)

Она ещё **молодая** женщина, но уже многого добилась в жизни.

She's still a **young** woman but has already achieved much in life.

677 - Тридцать ['tritsat'] - *Thirty*

На улице минус **тридцать** градусов.

It's minus **thirty** degrees outside.

678 - Роман [ra'man] - *A novel; a love affair*

Этот **роман** такой длинный! Я не уверена, что смогу дочитать его до конца.

This **novel** is so long! I'm not sure I'll be able to read it till the end.

679 - Требовать ['trebavat'] - *To demand, to require; to call for*

Ты не можешь **требовать** понимания, если сам не умеешь понимать.

You can't **demand** understanding if you yourself can't understand.

680 - Компания [kam'panija] - *A company (an enterprise)*

Наша **компания** быстро растёт.

Our **company** is growing fast.

681 - Частый ['tchastyj] - *Frequent*

Он **частый** гость в нашем доме.

He's a **frequent** guest in our house.

682 - Российский [ras'sijskij] - Russian (when referring to the country)

Российский рынок активно расширяется.
The **Russian** market is expanding actively.

683 - Рабочий [ra'botchij] - *A worker*

Мой дядя обычный **рабочий**, но с ним всегда интересно поговорить.
My uncle is an ordinary **worker** but it's always interesting to talk to him.

684 - Потерять [pate'rjat'] - *To lose*

Я всегда боюсь **потерять** паспорт, когда путешествую.
I'm always afraid **to lose** my passport when travelling.

685 - Течение [te'tchenije] - *A current; a tendency*

Течение горной реки было быстрым и шумным.
The **current** of the mountain river was fast and noisy.

686 - Синий ['sinij] - *Deep blue*

Я купила **синий** коврик для ванной.
I bought a **deep blue** mat for the bathroom.

687 - Столько ['stol'kə] - *So much/many*

Я **столько** хочу тебе рассказать.
There's **so much** I want to tell you.

688 - Тёплый ['tjeplyj] - *Warm*

Они поженились в **тёплый** июньский день.
They got married on a **warm** June day.

689 - Метр [metr] - *A meter/metre*

Она упала, когда до финиша оставался всего один **метр**.
She fell down when there was only one **meter** left to the finish line.

690 - Достать [das'tat'] - *To reach; to take out*

Я не могу **достать** коробку на верхней полке. Помоги мне, пожалуйста.
I can't **reach** the box on the top shelf. Help me, please.

691 - Железный [zhe'leznyj] - *Iron (adj)*

Дом окружал высокий **железный** забор.
The house was surrounded by a high **iron** fence.

692 - Институт [insti'tut] - *An institute; an institution*

Моя сестра поступила в медицинский **институт**.
My sister has entered a medical **institute**.

693 - Сообщить [saab'stchit'] - *To let know, to communicate*

Я обещаю **сообщить** тебе, если что-нибудь изменится.
I promise **to let** you **know** if anything changes.

694 - Интерес [inte'res] - *Interest*

Мой сын проявляет **интерес** к насекомым.
My son takes an **interest** in insects.

695 - Обычный [a'bychnyj] - *Usual, common, ordinary*

Это был **обычный** субботний день, но у меня было особое настроение.
That was a **usual** Saturday afternoon, but I had a special mood.

696 - Появляться [pajav'ljatsa] - *To show up; to appear*

Нам нельзя **появляться** на работе в джинсах.
We can't **show up** at work in jeans.

697 - Упасть [u'past'] - *To fall, to fall down*

Не спеши – дорога скользкая и ты можешь **упасть**.
Don't be in a hurry – the road is slippery and you can **fall**.

698 - Остальной [astəl''noj] - *Remaining, the rest of*

Мне нравится первый абзац, но **остальной** текст скучный.
I like the first paragraph but the **remaining** text is boring.

699 - Половина [pala'vina] - *A half*

Сейчас уже **половина** пятого.
It's **half** past four already.

700 - Московский [mas'kovskij] - *Moscow (acts like an adjective)*

Я люблю этот старый **московский** парк.
I like this old **Moscow** park.

701 - Шесть [shest'] - *Six*

Через **шесть** дней мы едем на море.
We're going to the seaside in **six** days.

702 - Получиться [palu'tchitsa] - *To be able to, to work out well (impersonal)*

У тебя должно **получиться** поладить с ними.
You should **be able to** get on well with them.

703 - Качество ['katchestvə] - *Quality; a feature*

Нас интересует **качество**, а не количество.
We're interested in **quality,** not in quantity.

704 - Бой [boj] - *A battle, a combat*

Это был страшный **бой**, и мы потеряли много солдат.
That was a terrible **battle** and we lost a lot of soldiers.

705 - Шея ['sheja] - *A neck*

Я всегда пользуюсь этой мазью, когда у меня болит **шея**.
I always use this ointment when my **neck** hurts.

706 - Вон [von] - *There (informal)*

Я вижу его. Он **вон** там.
I see him. He's over **there**.

707 - Идея [i'deja] - *An idea*

Это просто блестящая **идея**! Ты гений!
It's just a brilliant **idea**! You're a genius!

708 - Видимо ['vidimə] - *Apparently, evidently*

Ты, **видимо**, очень расстроилась из-за вашей ссоры.
You are **apparently** very upset because of your quarrel.

709 - Достаточно [das'tatəchnə] - *Enough, sufficiently*

Ты уверен, что мы купили **достаточно** напитков к вечеринке?
Are you sure that we've bought **enough** drinks for the party?

710 - Провести [praves'ti] - *To spend (perfective)*

Где вы планируете **провести** отпуск этим летом?
Where are you planning **to spend** your holiday this summer?

711 - Важно ['vazhnə] - It is important; importantly

Важно понимать, что у *людей разные вкусы*.

It is important to understand that people have different tastes.

712 - Трава [tra'va] - *Grass*

Трава перед домом пожелтела от жары.

The **grass** in front of the house turned yellow because of the heat.

713 - Дед [ded] - A grandfather; an old man (both informal)

Наш **дед** любил порядок и был очень строгим.

Our **grandfather** liked good order and was very strict.

714 - Сознание [saz'nanije] - *Consciousness*

Говорят, что духовные практики помогают расширить **сознание**.

They say that spiritual practices help to expand **consciousness**.

715 - Родитель [ra'ditel'] - *A parent*

Любой **родитель** переживает, когда дети болеют.

Any **parent** is worried when their kids are sick.

716 - Простить [pras'tit'] - *To forgive (perfective)*

Ты когда-нибудь сможешь меня **простить**?

Will you be ever able **to forgive** me?

717 - Бить ['bit'] - *To beat*

Нет никаких оправданий, чтобы **бить** *людей*.

There are no excuses **to beat** people.

718 - Чай [tchaj] - *Tea*

Утренний **чай** помогает мне проснуться даже лучше, чем кофе.

Morning **tea** helps me to wake up even better than coffee does.

719 - Поздний ['poznij] - *Late (adj)*

Это был **поздний** летний вечер со звёздным небом и тёплым ветром.

That was a **late** summer evening with a starry sky and a warm wind.

720 - Кивнуть [kiv'nut'] - *To nod*

Она попросила меня **кивнуть**, если я согласен на её предложение.

She asked me **to nod** if I agreed with her proposal.

721 - Род [rod] - *Race; generation*

Злодей в фильме хотел уничтожить весь человеческий **род**.

The villain in the movie wanted to destroy the whole human **race**.

722 - Исчезнуть [is'tcheznut'] - *To disappear, to vanish*

Мы обязательно найдем твою игрушку! Она не могла просто **исчезнуть**!

We'll surely find your toy! It couldn't just **disappear**!

723 - Тонкий ['tonkij] - *Thin*

Утром на озере появился **тонкий** слой льда.

A **thin** layer of ice appeared on the lake in the morning.

724 - Немецкий [ne'metskij] - *German; the German language*

Это очень надёжный **немецкий** инструмент.
It's a very reliable **German** tool.

725 - Звук [zvuk] - *A sound*

Я люблю **звук** дождя. Он помогает мне расслабиться.
I like the **sound** of the rain. It helps me to relax.

726 - Отдать [at'dat'] - *To give back, to return; to give away*

Девочка попросила подругу **отдать** её книгу к понедельнику.
The girl asked her friend **to give** her book **back** by Monday.

727 - Магазин [maga'zin] - *A shop*

Я иду в **магазин**. Тебе что-нибудь нужно?
I'm going to the **shop**. Do you need anything?

728 - Президент [prezi'dent] - *A president*

Наш **президент** управляет страной уже восемь лет.
Our **president** has been ruling the country for eight years already.

729 - Поэт [po'ɛt] - *A poet*

Этот молодой **поэт** уже достаточно хорошо известен.
This young **poet** is quite well-known already.

730 - Спасибо [spa'sibə] - *Thank you (for), thanks for*

Спасибо за полезный совет!
Thank you for the useful advice!

731 - Болезнь [ba'lezn'] - *A disease, an illness*

Рак – это ужасная **болезнь**, но её можно излечить.
Cancer is a terrible **disease** but it can be cured.

732 - Событие [sa'bytije] - *An event*

Рождение ребёнка – это радостное **событие** для всей семьи.
The birth of a child is a happy **event** for the whole family.

733 - Помочь [pa'motch] - *To help (perfective)*

Не уверен, смогу ли я **помочь**, но попытаюсь.
I'm not sure if I'll be able **to help** but I'll try.

734 - Кожа ['kozha] - *Skin; leather*

Её **кожа** обгорела на солнце.
Her **skin** has burnt in the sun.

735 - Лист [list] - *A leaf; a sheet*

Жёлтый **лист** в ручье напоминал парус.
The yellow **leaf** in the stream resembled a sail.

736 - Слать [slat'] - *To send*

Я обещаю **слать** письма как можно чаще.
I promise **to send** letters as often as possible.

737 - Вспоминать [vspami'nat'] - *To recall, to remember*

Мы любим **вспоминать** приятные моменты нашей жизни.
We like **to recall** the pleasant moments of our life.

738 - Прекрасный [prek'rasnyj] - *Beautiful, splendid*

Это **прекрасный** фотоальбом ручной работы.
It's a **beautiful** handmade photo album.

739 - Слеза [sle'za] - *A tear*

Каждая твоя **слеза** – трагедия для меня.
Every **tear** of yours is a tragedy for me.

740 - Надежда [na'dezhda] - *Hope*

Как говорят, **надежда** умирает последней.
As they say, **hope** dies last.

741 - Молча ['moltcha] - *Silently*

Он положил бумаги на стол и **молча** вышел из комнаты.
He put the papers on the table and left the room **silently**.

742 - Сильно ['sil'nə] - *Strongly, very much*

Он **сильно** сожалел о том, что порвал с ней.
He **strongly** regretted about breaking up with her.

743 - Верный ['vernyj] - *Faithful, loyal; true*

Этот пёс – мой самый **верный** друг.
This dog is my most **faithful** friend.

744 - Литература [litera'tura] - *Literature*

Иностранная **литература** была моим любимым предметом в университете.
Foreign **literature** used to be my favorite subject at university.

745 - Оружие [a'ruzhije] - *Weapon(s), arms*

Он незаконно хранил **оружие** и был арестован за это.
He stored **weapons** illegally and was arrested for it.

746 - Готовый [ga'tovyj] - *Ready, prepared*

Нам нужен веб-сайт, полностью **готовый** к работе.
We need a **ready**-to-use website.

747 - Запах ['zapah] - *A smell*

Я ненавижу **запах** рыбы.
I hate the **smell** of fish.

748 - Неожиданно [nea'zhidannə] - *Unexpectedly*

Зима оказалась **неожиданно** холодной.
The winter turned out to be **unexpectedly** cold.

749 - Вчера [vche'ra] - *Yesterday*

Вчера мы наконец-то закончили ремонт спальни.
Yesterday we finally finished the renovation of the bedroom.

750 - Вздохнуть [vzdah'nut'] - *To sigh; to take a breath (perfective)*

Что заставило тебя так грустно **вздохнуть**?
What made you **sigh** so sadly?

751 - Роль [rol'] - *A role, a part*

Она получила главную **роль** в новом фильме.
She got a starring **role** in a new film.

752 - Рост [rost] - *Growth; height*

Рост цен на нефть снизился в этом году.
This year the **growth** of oil price has decreased.

753 - Природа [pri'roda] - *Nature*

Весной **природа** просыпается после зимнего сна.
In spring, **nature** wakes up after the winter sleep.

754 - Политический [pali'titcheskij] - *Political*

Политический климат в стране ухудшился.
The **political** climate in the country has gotten worse.

755 - Точка ['tochka] - *A point; a dot*

Это событие – стартовая **точка** конфликта.
This event is the starting **point** of the conflict.

756 - Звезда [zvez'da] - *A star*

Люди говорят, что падающая **звезда** может осуществить желание.

People say that a shooting **star** can make a wish come true.

757 - Петь [pet'] - *To sing*

Многие люди любят **петь** в душе.

Many people like **to sing** in the shower.

758 - Садиться [sa'ditsa] - *To sit down*

На эту скамейку нельзя **садиться** – она окрашена.

One can't **sit down** on this bench – it's been painted.

759 - Фамилия [fa'milija] - *A surname, last name*

Я не могу понять, кто он по национальности, а его **фамилия** ни о чём не говорит.

I can't understand what his nationality is and his **surname** doesn't say anything.

760 - Характер [ha'rachter] - *Character, temper*

Она очень красивая девушка, но её **характер** всё портит.

She's a very beautiful girl but her **character** spoils everything.

761 - Пожалуйста [pa'zhalusta] - *Please; you are welcome*

Пожалуйста, перестаньте шуметь.

Please, stop making noise.

762 - Выше ['vyshe] - *Higher*

Зимой наши расходы **выше**.

Our outgoings are **higher** in winter.

763 - Офицер [afi'tser] - *An officer (military)*

Офицер повёл себя как настоящий герой.
The **officer** behaved like a true hero.

764 - Толпа [tol'pa] - *A crowd*

Перед посольством собралась **толпа** людей.
A **crowd** of people gathered in front of the embassy.

765 - Перестать [pere'stat'] - *To stop, to cease*

Я не могу **перестать** думать о тебе.
I can't **stop** thinking about you.

766 - Придтись [prid'tis'] - *To fall on (a date) (a variation of 'прийтись')*

В этом году мой день рождения должен **придтись** на вторник.
My birthday should **fall on** Tuesday this year.

767 - Уровень ['urəven'] - *A level*

Уровень образованности в стране повысился.
The **level** of education in the country has increased.

768 - Неизвестный [neiz'vesnyj] - *Unknown*

Космос – это другой, **неизвестный** мир.
Space is a different **unknown** world.

769 - Кресло ['kreslə] - *An armchair*

Мы купили красивое винтажное **кресло**.
We've bought a beautiful vintage **armchair**.

770 - Баба ['baba] - Colloquial, sometimes with a rude connotation for 'woman', 'broad'

Кто эта **баба**, с которой ты сидел в кафе?
Who's that **broad** you were sitting with in a cafe?

771 - Секунда [se'kunda] - *A second*

Мне нужна всего лишь **секунда** вашего времени.
I need just one **second** of your time.

772 - Пожаловать [pa'zhaləvat'] - Most often used in a set expression 'Добро пожаловать!' - Welcome!; to grant

Дамы и господа, **добро пожаловать** на наш ежегодный фестиваль!
Ladies and gentlemen, **welcome** to our annual festival!

773 - Банк [bank] - *A bank*

Во время кризиса этот **банк** потерял много клиентов.
This **bank** lost lots of clients during the crisis.

774 - Опыт ['opyt] - Experience; an experiment

Опыт работы в продажах помог ему получить работу.
The **experience** of working in sales helped him get the job.

775 - Тихий ['tihij] - *Quiet, still*

Тихий звук скрипки создал очень приятную атмосферу.
The **quiet** sound of the violin created a very pleasant atmosphere.

776 - Поскольку [pas'kolku] - *Since*

Поскольку эта машина очень дорогая, мы возьмём кредит.
Since this car is very expensive we'll take a loan.

777 - Сапог [sa'pog] - *A boot*

Посмотри, твой левый **сапог** весь в грязи.
Look, your left **boot** is all covered in mud.

778 - Правило ['pravilo] - *A rule*

Это грамматическое **правило** очень простое.
This grammar **rule** is very simple.

779 - Стекло [stek'lo] - *Glass*

А вы знали, что **стекло** делают из песка?
Did you know that **glass** is made of sand?

780 - Получать [palu'chat'] - *To receive, to get*

Я буду **получа**ть твою почту, пока ты будешь в командировке.
I'll **receive** your mail while you're on a business trip.

781 - Внутренний ['vnutrennij] - *Inner*

Внутренний мир человека – это загадка.
A person's **inner** world is a mystery.

782 - Дочь [dotch] - *A daughter*

Наша **дочь** заканчивает школу в этом году.
Our **daughter** graduates from school this year.

783 - Называться [nazy'vatsa] - **To be called; to be named (impersonal)**

Наш ресторан будет **называться** "Мелодия".
Our restaurant is going **to be called** 'Melody'.

784 - Надеяться [na'dejatsa] - *To hope*

Доктор сказал, что мы можем **надеяться** на её скорое выздоровление.
The doctor said that we could **hope** for her quick recovery.

785 - Член [tchlen] - **A member; colloquial for penis**

Он **член** влиятельной международной организации.
He's **a member** of an influential international organisation.

786 - Протянуть [pratja'nut'] - *To reach out; to hold out*

Фокусник попросил меня **протянуть** руку и закрыть глаза.
The illusionist asked me **to reach out** my hand and close my eyes.

787 - Государственный [gasu'darsvennyj] - *State (adj)*

Этот **государственный** институт отвечает за поддержку семей с детьми.
This **state** institution is responsible for the support of families with children.

788 - Десяток [de'sjatək] - *A dozen (literally means 10)*

Утро только началось, а я уже получил с **десяток** деловых звонков.
The morning has just begun and I've already received about **a dozen** business calls.

789 - Глубокий [glu'bokij] - *Deep (adj)*

Этот ручей не **глубокий**, и мы можем легко перейти его.
This stream isn't **deep** and we can easily cross it.

790 - Цветок [tsve'tok] - *A flower*

На конверте был нарисован нежный розовый **цветок**.
A tender pink **flower** was painted on the envelope.

791 - Ах [ah] - *Ah!, oh!*

Ах, какой прекрасный букет!
Ah, what a wonderful bouquet!

792 - Желание [zhe'lanije] - *A wish, desire*

Загадай **желание** и никому не рассказывай, а то не сбудется!
Make **a wish** and don't tell anyone or else it won't come true!

793 - Дождь [dozhd'] - *Rain*

Дождь был таким сильным, что затопил улицы.
The **rain** was so hard that it flooded the streets.

794 - Впереди [vpere'di] - *Ahead; in front of*

У нас столько счастливых дней **впереди**!
We've got so many happy days **ahead**!

795 - Подходить [padha'dit'] - *To fit, to suit, to match; to come up to*

Этот размер не может тебе **подходить** – ты гораздо выше.
This size can't **fit** you – you're much taller.

796 - Много ['mnogə] - *Much, many, a lot of*

У меня не **много** времени, так что давайте перейдём к делу.
I don't have **much** time so let's get down to business.

797 - Лоб [lob] - *A forehead*

Его **лоб** был покрыт капельками пота.
His **forehead** was covered with drops of sweat.

798 - Улыбка [u'lybka] - *A smile*

У неё была солнечная **улыбка** и добрые глаза.
She had a sunny **smile** and kind eyes.

799 - Борьба [bar''ba] - *Struggle, fight*

Борьба с самим собой – самая сложная **борьба**.
The **struggle** against yourself is the most difficult **struggle**.

800 - Ворот ['vorət] - *A collar*

Ворот его рубашки был мокрым и грязным.
The **collar** of his shirt was wet and dirty.

801 - Ящик ['jastchik] - *A box; a drawer*

Мальчик спрятал **ящик** со своими сокровищами под кроватью.
The boy hid **a box** with his treasures under the bed.

802 - Этаж [ɛ'tazh] - *A floor, a storey*

Первый **этаж** нашего дома был построен за неделю.
The first **floor** of our house was built within a week.

803 - Служить [slu'zhit'] - *To serve, to serve as*

После школы он собирался **служить** в армии.
After school, he was going **to serve** in the army.

804 - Вновь [vnof'] - *Again, anew (literary style)*

Мы **вновь** собрались здесь, чтобы вспомнить великого поэта.
We gathered here **again** to recall the great poet.

805 - Голубой [galu'boj] - *Blue; gay*

Этот **голубой** галстук не подходит к коричневому ремню.
This **blue** tie doesn't match the brown belt.

806 - Нечего ['netchego] - *There is nothing to*

Ему **нечего** делать, и он умирает от скуки.
There is nothing for him **to** do and he's dying of boredom.

807 - Революция [reva'lutsija] - *A revolution*

Мне кажется, что любая **революция** – это очень агрессивный метод.

It seems to me that any **revolution** is a very aggressive method.

808 - Впервые [fper'vyje] - *For the first time*

Когда мне было шесть, я **впервые** увидела настоящий водопад.

When I was six I saw a real waterfall **for the first time**.

809 - Сосед [sa'sed] - *A neighbor*

Мой **сосед** редко устраивает шумные вечеринки.

My **neighbor** rarely makes noisy parties.

810 - Сестра [ses'tra] - *A sister*

Его **сестра** вегетарианка.

His **sister** is a vegetarian.

811 - Долгий ['dolgij] - *Long*

У нас был **долгий** разговор о наших отношениях.

We had a **long** talk about our relationship.

812 - Чей [tchej] - *Whose*

Вы не знаете, **чей** это зонт?

Do you know **whose** umbrella it is?

813 - Поверить [pa'verit'] - *To believe (perfective)*

Я не могу **поверить**, что ты выиграла в лотерею.

I can't **believe** that you've won the lottery.

814 - Ситуация [situ'atsija] - *A situation*

Ситуация сложная, но я знаю, что делать.
The **situation** is difficult but I know what to do.

815 - Взглянуть [vzglja'nut'] - *To have a look, to glance*

Детям было любопытно **взглянуть** на новорождённых щенков.
The children were curious **to have a look** at the newborn puppies.

816 - Слабый ['slabyj] - *Weak, feeble*

Пока мой папа болел, он был такой **слабый**, что едва мог есть сам.
When my father was sick he was so **weak** that he could barely eat himself.

817 - Количество [ka'litchestvə] - *Number, quantity, amount*

В этом году **количество** выпускников, проваливших тест, уменьшилось.
The **number** of graduates who failed the test decreased this year.

818 - Вызывать [vyzy'vat'] - *To cause; to call*

Арахис может **вызывать** аллергию у некоторых людей.
Peanuts can **cause** allergy in some people.

819 - Уверенный [u'verennyj] - *Confident, sure*

Я изменил своё мнение, когда увидел его **уверенный** взгляд.
I changed my mind when I saw his **confident** look.

820 - Выход ['vyhəd] - *A way out; an exit*

Мы должны подумать и найти **выход** из этой ситуации.
We must think and find **a way out** of this situation.

821 - Совет [sa'vet] - *Advice*

Его **совет** помог мне принять правильное решение.

His **advice** helped me take the right decision.

822 - Дурак [du'rak] - *A fool, an idiot*

Ты такой **дурак**, что упустил эту возможность!

You are such **a fool** to have missed this opportunity!

823 - Любимый [lju'bimyj] - *Favorite*

Рождество – мой **любимый** праздник.

Christmas is my **favorite** holiday.

824 - Союз [sa'juz] - *A union; an alliance*

Европейский **Союз** поддерживает беженцев из восточных стран.

The European **Union** supports refugees from eastern countries.

825 - Лето ['letə] - *Summer*

Прошлое **лето** было дождливым и прохладным.

The last **summer** was rainy and cool.

826 - Ожидать [azhi'dat'] - *To expect, to anticipate*

Вы можете **ожидать**, что перевод будет готов к среде.

You can **expect** the translation to be ready by Wednesday.

827 - Огород [aga'rod] - *A vegetable garden*

Здорово иметь свой **огород**! Все овощи натуральные и свежие.

It's great to have your own **vegetable garden**! All the vegetables are natural and fresh.

828 - Висеть [vi'set'] - *To hang*

Почему твоё платье лежит на полу? Оно должно **висеть** в шкафу.

Why is your dress lying on the floor? It must **hang** in the wardrobe.

829 - Граница [gra'nitsa] - *A border; a boundary*

Граница между двумя государствами расположена вдоль реки.

The **border** between the two states is situated along a river.

830 - Цвет [tsvet] - *A color*

Цвет глаз может сказать что-нибудь о человеке?

Can the **color** of the eyes say anything about the person?

831 - Серьёзный [serjeznyj] - *Serious, earnest*

Для школьника он очень **серьёзный** и спокойный.

He's very **serious** and calm for a schoolboy.

832 - Создать [saz'dat'] - *To create*

С помощью этой программы легко **создать** новый проект.

With the help of this program it's easy **to create** a new project.

833 - Интересный [inte'resnyj] - *Interesting*

Это очень **интересный** роман! Я прочёл его за три дня!

It's a very **interesting** novel! I read it in three days!

834 - Свобода [sva'boda] - *Freedom*

Свобода слова важна для развития демократического общества.

Freedom of speech is important for the development of democratic society.

835 - Зато [za'to] - *On the other hand*

Он не зарабатывает много, но **зато** много времени проводит с семьёй.

He doesn't earn much but **on the other hand** he spends much time with his family.

836 - Стул [stul] - *A chair*

Я предложил посетителю **стул**, но он отказался.

I offered the visitor **a chair** but he refused.

837 - Уехать [u'jehat'] - *To leave, to go away; to drive off (perfective)*

Она решила **уехать** из страны и начать новую жизнь.

She decided **to leave** the country and start a new life.

838 - Поезд ['poezd] - *A train*

Наш **поезд** прибывает ровно в пять.

Our **train** arrives at five sharp.

839 - Музыка ['muzyka] - *Music*

Классическая **музыка** не для меня. Я её не понимаю.

Classical **music** is not for me. I don't understand it.

840 - Тень [ten'] - *Shade; a shadow*

В солнечный день нелегко найти **тень**.

It's not easy to find **shade** on a sunny day.

841 - Лошадь ['loshat'] - *A horse*

Моя внучка всегда хотела иметь **лошадь**.

My granddaughter has always wanted to have **a horse**.

842 - Поле ['pole] - *A field*

За домом было большое пшеничное **поле**.

There was a big **field** of wheat behind the house.

843 - Выглядеть ['vygljadet'] - To look (to have an appearance, not the process of watching)

Она всегда старается модно **выглядеть**.

She always tries **to look** fashionable.

844 - Учиться [u'tchitsa] - *To study*

Ты должен усердно **учиться**, если хочешь поступить в университет.

You must **study** hard if you want to enter a university.

845 - Левый ['levyj] - *Left, left-hand*

Посмотри, твой **левый** карман порван.

Look, your **left** pocket is torn.

846 - Разговаривать [razga'varivat'] - To talk, to speak, to converse (with)

Мы с сестрой можем часами **разговаривать** друг с другом.

My sister and I can **talk** to each other for hours.

847 - Детский ['detskij] - *Child's, child (as an adj)*

Детский смех делает жизнь счастливее.

A child's laughter makes life happier.

848 - Тип [tip] - A type, a kind; slang for 'dude', 'guy'

Какой **тип** счёта Вы хотите открыть?

What **type** of account do you want to open?

849 - Суд [sud] - *Court; judgement*

Суд постановил, что он не виновен.
The **court** stated that he's not guilty.

850 - Связанный ['svjazannyj] - *Connected (with)*

Я нашла файл, **связанный** с твоим делом.
I've found a file **connected** with your case.

851 - Горячий [gar'jatchij] - *Hot*

Будь осторожен – чайник **горячий**!
Be careful – the kettle is **hot**!

852 - Площадь ['plostchad'] - *A square (open space in a town or a city); an area*

Это историческое место города – **площадь** Свободы.
It's an historical place of the city – **Freedom** Square.

853 - Помогать [pama'gat'] - *To help*

Настоящие друзья должны всегда **помогать** друг другу.
True friends should always **help** each other.

854 - Счастливый [stchas'livyj] - *Happy*

Я помню тот **счастливый** день, когда родился мой внук.
I remember that **happy** day when my grandson was born.

855 - Повернуться [paver'nutsa] - *To turn around*

Я понял, что мне лучше **повернуться** и уйти.
I realized that I'd better **turn around** and leave.

856 - Позволить [paz'volit'] - *To afford; to allow, to permit*

В этом году мы не можем **позволить** себе отпуск за границей.
This year we can't **afford** a holiday abroad.

857 - Встретить ['vstretit'] - *To meet, to encounter*

Я не ожидал **встретить** её в этом незнакомом городе.
I didn't expect **to meet** her in that unfamiliar town.

858 - Радость ['radost'] - *Joy*

Это большая **радость** – встретиться снова после стольких лет.
It's a great **joy** to meet again after so many years.

859 - Острый ['ostryj] - *Sharp; acute*

Нож был очень **острый**, и я порезался.
The knife was very **sharp** and I cut myself.

860 - Возраст ['vozrast] - *Age*

Его **возраст** совсем не соответствует его внешности.
His **age** doesn't correspond to his appearance at all.

861 - Орган ['organ] - *An organ (anatomy)*

Печень – это **орган**, который работает как фильтр.
The **liver** is an organ that works as a filter.

862 - Карта ['karta] - *A map*

Карта была неправильной, и мы заблудились.
The **map** was incorrect and we lost our way.

863 - Входить [vha'dit'] - *To enter, to go into; to be included in*

Нельзя **входить** в чью-либо комнату, не постучавшись.
One can't **enter** anybody's room without knocking.

864 - Обнаружить [abna'ruzhit'] - *To find, to find out*

Я был удивлён **обнаружить** мобильный сестры в своём рюкзаке.
I was surprised **to find** my sister's mobile in my backpack.

865 - Король [ka'rol'] - *A king*

Старый **король** был справедливым и мудрым.
The old **king** was just and wise.

866 - Слава ['slava] - *Fame*

Слава и деньги часто портят людей.
Fame and money often spoil people.

867 - Полковник [pal'kovnik] - *A colonel (military)*

Полковник был одиноким человеком без семьи и детей.
The **colonel** was a lonely man without a family and kids.

868 - Мелкий ['melkij] - **Little, small, minute; shallow**

Мелкий дождь и холодная погода ещё больше ухудшили моё настроение.
The **little** rain and the cold weather made my mood even worse.

869 - Бок [bok] - *A side*

Ветеринар попросил меня перевернуть собаку на левый **бок**.
The vet asked me to turn the dog on its left **side**.

870 - Цена [tse'na] - *Price*

Цена этого костюма вполне разумная.
The **price** of this suit is quite reasonable.

871 - Информация [infar'matsija] - *Information*

Эта **информация** очень полезна для нашего исследования.
This **information** is very useful for our research.

872 - Мозг [mosk] - *Brain*

Сегодня мой **мозг** просто отказывается работать.
My **brain** simply refuses to work today.

873 - Удовольствие [uda'vol'stvije] - *A pleasure*

Слушать эту музыку вживую – **удовольствие**.
Listening to this music live is **a pleasure**.

874 - Воля ['volja] - Will, willpower; freedom

Его сильная **воля** помогла ему добиться своей цели.
His strong **will** helped him achieve his goal.

875 - Область ['oblast'] - A region, a province; a sphere

Эта **область** страны богата лесами и озёрами.
This **region** of the country is rich in forests and lakes.

876 - Крыша ['krysha] - *A roof*

Крыша нашего загородного дома течёт, и мы будем менять её.
The **roof** of our country house is leaking and we're going to fix it.

877 - Нести [nes'ti] - *To carry*

Она не может сама **нести** эти сумки. Помоги ей.
She can't **carry** these bags herself. Help her.

878 - Обратно [ab'ratnə] - *Back*

Мы не довольны качеством и хотим наши деньги **обратно**.
We're not happy with the quality and want our money **back**.

879 - Современный [savre'mennyj] - *Modern, contemporary*

Современный мир меняется быстрее, чем век назад.
The **modern** world changes faster than a century ago.

880 - Дама ['dama] - *A lady*

Эта пожилая **дама** много помогает бездомным.
This elderly **lady** helps the homeless a lot.

881 - Семь [sem'] - *Seven*

Многие считают, что **семь** – это магическое число.
Many people consider **seven** to be a magical number.

882 - Весёлый [ves'jolyj] - *Merry, cheerful, happy*

Весёлый клоун принёс детям много радости.
The **merry** clown brought the children much joy.

883 - Прислать [pris'lat'] - **To send (to, to this place) (perfective)**

Я обещаю **прислать** тебе открытку, когда буду на курорте.
I promise **to send** you a postcard when I'm at the resort.

884 - Сад [sad] - **A garden, an orchard**

Папа много работает, чтобы наш **сад** был таким красивым.
Dad works a lot for our **garden** to be so beautiful.

885 - Правительство [pra'vitel'stvə] - *A government*

Новое **правительство** менее популярно среди народа.
The new **government** is less popular with people.

886 - Милый ['milyj] - *Cute*

Этот щенок такой **милый**! Давай оставим его!
This puppy is so **cute**! Let's keep it!

887 - Относиться [atnə'sitsa] - *To treat*

Постарайся **относиться** к ней с пониманием.
Try **to treat** her with understanding.

888 - Возникать [vazni'kat'] - *To arise, to emerge*

При решении этой задачи могут **возникать** некоторые вопросы.
While solving this task, some questions may **arise**.

889 - Мол [mol] - He says, they say (colloquial)

Они не одолжили мне денег, потому что я, **мол**, слишком мало зарабатываю.

They didn't lend me any money because **they say** I earn too little.

890 - Повторить [pavta'rit'] - *To repeat*

Учитель попросил учеников **повторить** последнее предложение.

The teacher asked the pupils **to repeat** the last sentence.

891 - Название [naz'vanije] - *A name, a title*

Ты помнишь **название** того блюда, что мы готовили на прошлой неделе?

Do you remember the **name** of the dish we cooked last week?

892 - Средний ['srednij] - *Average; middle*

Каков **средний** доход по стране в этом месяце?
What's the **average** income across the country this month?

893 - Пример [pri'mer] - *An example*

Ты можешь привести **пример**, чтобы я лучше понял правило?
Can you give an **example** so that I understand the rule better?

894 - Невозможно [nevaz'mozhnə] - *It is impossible*

Невозможно быть успешным, не прилагая никаких усилий.
It is impossible to be successful without making any effort.

895 - Зеркало ['zerkalə] - *A mirror*

Я купила это красивое **зеркало** на распродаже.
I bought this beautiful **mirror** at a sale.

896 - Погибнуть [pa'gibnut'] - To be killed, to perish (to die of unnatural causes)

Мы не верили, что он мог **погибнуть** в автокатастрофе.
We didn't believe that he could **be killed** in a car crash.

897 - Американский [ameri'kanskij] - *American*

У неё сильный **американский** акцент.
She's got a strong **American** accent.

898 - Дым [dym] - *Smoke*

Я терпеть не могу сигаретный **дым**.
I can't stand cigarette **smoke**.

899 - Гореть [ga'ret'] - *To burn*

Эта большая свеча может **гореть** до пяти часов.
This big candle can **burn** up to five hours.

900 - Плакать ['plakat'] - *To cry, to weep*

Я не могу не **плакать** когда смотрю эту сцену из фильма.
I can't help but **cry** when watching this movie scene.

901 - Весьма [ves''ma] - *Rather, quite*

Мой дедушка был **весьма** хорошо образован для своего времени.
My grandfather was **rather** well-educated for his time.

902 - Факт [fakt] - *A fact*

Тот **факт**, что я не замужем, меня совсем не беспокоит.
The **fact** that I'm not married doesn't bother me at all.

903 - Двигаться ['dvigatsa] - *To move*

Как ты заставляешь эти картинки **двигаться**?
How do you make these pictures **move**?

904 - Рыба ['ryba] - *Fish*

Эта **рыба** не водится в солёной воде.
This **fish** is not found in salty water.

905 - Добавить [da'bavit'] - *To add*

Попробуй **добавить** в суп немного больше перца.
Try **to add** a bit more pepper to the soup.

906 - Удивиться [udi'vitsa] - *To be surprised, to wonder at*

Ты можешь **удивиться**, но я уже всё знаю.
You may **be surprised** but I already know everything.

907 - Бабушка ['babushka] - *A grandmother*

Моя **бабушка** готовит лучше любого шеф-повара.
My **grandmother** cooks better than any chef.

908 - Вино [vi'no] - *Wine*

Я предпочитаю полусухое **вино**.
I prefer semidry **wine**.

909 - Ибо ['ibə] - For, since, as (literary, has an ironical connotation if used in everyday speech)

Мы не остановимся, **ибо** наша борьба священна.
We shall not stop **for** our struggle is sacred.

910 - Учитель [u'tchitel'] - *A teacher*

Хороший **учитель** должен быть творческим человеком.
A good **teacher** must be a creative person.

911 - Действовать ['dejstvavat'] - *To act*

Врачи должны были **действовать** быстро, чтобы спасти ему жизнь.

The doctors had **to act** fast to save his life.

912 - Осторожно [asta'rozhnə] - *Carefully*

Она взяла кристальный шар и **осторожно** положила его в коробку.

She took the crystal ball and put it into the box **carefully**.

913 - Круг [krug] - *A circle; a range*

Круг – символ бесконечности.
The **circle** is a symbol of infinity.

914 - Папа ['papa] - *Dad*

Наш **папа** часто брал нас с собой на рыбалку.
Our **dad** often took us fishing with him.

915 - Правильно ['pravil'nə] - *Correctly*

Он ответил **правильно** на все вопросы и сдал тест.
He answered all the questions **correctly** and passed the test.

916 - Недавно [ne'davnə] - *Recently, lately*

Я видела его **недавно**, и он ничуть не изменился.
I've seen him **recently** and he hasn't changed a bit.

917 - Держаться [der'zhatsa] - *To hold on, to hold on to*

Я знаю, нам всем тяжело, но мы должны **держаться**.
I know it's hard for all of us but we must **hold on**.

918 - Причём [pri'tchjom] - *Moreover, with*

Эти близнецы окончили один университет, **причём** оба работают в одном месте.

These twins graduated from the same university, **moreover** both work at the same place.

919 - Лететь [le'tet'] - *To fly*

Крыло птицы было сломано, и она не могла **лететь**.

The bird's wing was broken and it couldn't **fly**.

920 - Носить [na'sit'] - *To wear; to carry*

Я всегда стараюсь **носить** шляпу в жаркую погоду.

I always try **to wear** a hat in hot weather.

921 - Повод ['povəd] - *A reason, an excuse*

Тебе не нужно искать **повод**, чтобы позвонить мне.

You needn't find **a reason** to call me.

922 - Лагерь ['lager'] - *A camp*

Она поехала в летний **лагерь** на каникулах.

She went to a summer **camp** on holidays.

923 - Птица ['ptitsa] - *A bird*

Попугай – единственная **птица**, которая может говорить.

The parrot is the only **bird** that can talk.

924 - Корабль [ka'rabl'] - *A ship*

Этот старый **корабль** в основном используется для экскурсий вдоль берега.

This old **ship** is mostly used for excursions along the shore.

925 - Мнение ['mnenije] - *An opinion*

Твоё **мнение** много значит для меня.
Your **opinion** means a lot to me.

926 - Ночной [natcth'noj] - *Night, nighttime (adj)*

Твой **ночной** звонок напугал меня.
Your **night** call frightened me.

927 - Здоровый [zda'rovyj] - *Healthy*

Овсянка с молоком – это **здоровый** завтрак.
Oats with milk is a **healthy** breakfast.

928 - Зима [zi'ma] - *Winter*

Зима – время семейных праздников и волшебства.
Winter is the time of family holidays and magic.

929 - Сухой [su'hoj] - *Dry*

Сухой климат хорошо влияет на моё здоровье.
Dry climates have a good influence on my health.

930 - Километр [kila'metr] - *A kilometer*

До заправки всего один **километр**.
There's only one **kilometer** to the filling station.

931 - Кровать [kra'vat'] - *A bed*

Наша новая **кровать** более просторная.
Our new **bed** is more spacious.

932 - Привыкнуть [pri'vyknut'] - *To get used to*

Я не могу **привыкнуть** делать зарядку по утрам.
I can't **get used to** doing morning exercises.

933 - Прочее ['protcheje] - *So on, so forth*

Здесь я храню всякие мелочи: серёжки, кольца и **прочее**.
Here I keep different little things: earrings, rings, and **so on**.

934 - Свободный [sva'bodnyj] - *Free; vacant*

Свободный человек не зависит от мнения других людей.
A **free** person doesn't depend on the opinion of other people.

935 - Лестница ['lesnitsa] - *Stairs; a ladder*

Эта **лестница** старая и всё время скрипит.
These **stairs** are old and are creaking all the time.

936 - Неужели [neu'zheli] - *Really (to express surprise)*

Мама, **неужели** эта девочка на фото – это ты?
Mom, is this girl in the photo **really** you?

937 - Обязательно [abja'zatel'nə] - *Necessarily*

Иметь образование не **обязательно** значит быть умным.
Having an education doesn't **necessarily** mean being clever.

938 - Вверх [vverh] - *Up, upwards*

Мы шли **вверх** по холму более двух часов и очень устали.
We'd been walking **up** the hill for more than two hours and were very tired.

939 - Детство ['detstvə] - *Childhood*

Моё **детство** ассоциируется у меня с теплом и радостью.
I associate my **childhood** with warmth and joy.

940 - Остров ['ostrəv] - *An island*

Когда я был маленьким мальчиком, я мечтал попасть на необитаемый **остров**.
When I was a little boy I dreamt of getting to an uninhabited **island**.

941 - Статья [stat''ja] - *An article*

Эта **статья** о детском доме сильно впечатлила меня.
That **article** about an orphanage impressed me a lot.

942 - Позвонить [pazva'nit'] - *To call (by phone), (perfect)*

Не забудь **позвонить** мне, когда вернёшься домой.
Don't forget **to call** me when you return home.

943 - Столь [stol'] - So, such (literary style)

Его цели были **столь** амбициозными, что никто не верил в его успех.
His goals were **so** ambitious that nobody believed in his success.

944 - Мешать [me'shat'] - To bother, to prevent; to stir

Дети, постарайтесь не **мешать** мне, пока я работаю.
Kids, try not to **to bother** me while I'm working.

945 - Водка ['vodka] - *Vodka*

Водка – это крепкий алкогольный напиток.
Vodka is a strong alcoholic beverage.

946 - Темнота [temna'ta] - *Darkness*

Темнота пугает многих людей.
Darkness frightens many people.

947 - Возникнуть [vaz'niknut'] - *To arise, to emerge (perfective)*

При решении этой задачи могут **возникнуть** различные вопросы.

While solving this task, different questions may **arise**.

948 - Способный [spa'sobnyj] - *Capable, able*

Нам нужен человек, **способный** решить эту проблему самостоятельно.

We need a person who's **capable** of solving this problem independently.

949 - Станция ['stantsija] - *A station*

Эта железнодорожная **станция** закрыта на ремонт.
This railway **station** is closed for repairs.

950 - Желать [zhe'lat'] - *To wish, to desire*

У меня есть всё. Я не могу **желать** большего.
I've got everything. I can't **wish** for more.

951 - Попробовать [pap'robavat'] - *To try; to taste (to test the flavor of something) (perfective)*

Я хочу **попробовать** выучить ещё один иностранный язык.
I want **to try** to learn another foreign language.

952 - Получаться [palu'tchatsa] - *To be able to, to work out well*

Со временем это упражнение будет **получаться** у тебя всё лучше и лучше.

With time you will **be able to** do this exercise better and better.

953 - Гражданин [grəzhda'nin] - *A citizen*

Каждый **гражданин** имеет право на отдых.
Every **citizen** has the right to rest.

954 - Странно ['strannə] - *Weirdly, strangely*

Что случилось? Ты ведёшь себя **странно**.
What's happened? You behave **weirdly**.

955 - Вскоре ['vskore] - *Soon (a more literary variant of 'скоро')*

Вскоре они совсем забыли о своей ссоре.
Soon they forgot about their argument.

956 - Команда [ka'manda] - *A team, a crew; an order*

Наша футбольная **команда** проиграла в финальном матче.
Our football **team** lost in the final match.

957 - Заболевание [zabale'vanije] - *A disease, a sickness*

Учёные научились контролировать это **заболевание**.
Scientists learned to control this **disease**.

958 - Живот [zhi'vot] - *Belly, stomach*

Мой толстый **живот** меня раздражает! Я хочу похудеть.
My fat **belly** irritates me! I want to lose weight.

959 - Ставить [s'tavit'] - *To put, to place*

Я часто забываю **ставить** вещи обратно на свои места.
I often forget **to put** things back to their places.

960 - Ради ['radi] - *For the sake of*

Они решили не разводиться **ради** детей.
They decided not to get divorced **for the sake of** the children.

961 - Тишина [tishi'na] - *Silence, quietness*

Мне нужна полная **тишина,** чтобы сосредоточиться.
I need complete **silence** to concentrate.

962 - Понятно [pa'njatnə] - *Clearly*

Ты не умеешь **понятно** объяснять – я ничего не понимаю.
You aren't able to explain **clearly** – I don't understand anything.

963 - Фронт [front] - *A front (military)*

Во время Второй мировой войны даже подростки уходили на **фронт.**
During World War II even teenagers went to the **front.**

964 - Щека [stche'ka] - *A cheek*

После укуса её **щека** некоторое время оставалась красной.
After the sting her **cheek** remained red for some time.

965 - Страшно ['strashnə] - **One is scared (with the pronoun in dative case); scary**

Мне **страшно!** Включи свет!
I **am scared!** Turn on the light!

966 - Район [ra'jon] - *A district; an area*

Этот **район** самый густонаселённый в городе.
This **district** is the most densely populated one in the city.

967 - Наверно [na'vernə] - *Probably, likely*

Он, **наверно,** проспал. Вчера он очень поздно вернулся домой.
He **probably** overslept. He came back home very late yesterday.

968 - Проводить [prava'dit'] - *To spend, to pass*

Я люблю **проводить** время с родственниками.

I like **to spend** time with my relatives.

969 - Выражение [vyra'zhenije] - *An expression*

Выражение её лица объясняло всё без слов.

The **expression** on her face explained everything without words.

970 - Слегка [sleh'ka] - *Slightly, a bit*

Наши планы на лето **слегка** изменились.

Our plans for the summer have changed **slightly**.

971 - Мешок [me'shok] - *A sack*

Он принёс целый **мешок** подарков.

He brought a whole **sack** of presents.

972 - Обещать [obe'stchat'] - *To promise*

Я не могу **обещать** тебе, что починю твою машину, но я попробую.

I can't **promise** you to repair your car but I'll try.

973 - Дорогой [dara'goj] - *Expensive; dear*

Этот кожаный кошелёк слишком **дорогой** для меня.

This leather purse is too **expensive** for me.

974 - Судить [su'dit'] - *To judge*

Я стараюсь не **судить** людей по внешности.

I try not to **judge** people by appearance.

975 - Большинство [bal'shinst'vo] - *Majority, most*

Большинство студентов приняли участие в конкурсе.

The **majority** of the students took part in the contest.

976 - Собраться [sab'ratsa] - To gather, to assemble (perfective)

Мы решили **собраться** после работы и обсудить планы на выходные.

We decided **to gather** after work and to discuss the plans for the weekend.

977 - Управление [uprav'lenije] - *Administration, managing*

Эффективное **управление** любой работой влияет на результат.

Efficient **administration** of any work influences the result.

978 - Колоть [ka'lot'] - To chop (firewood); to prick

Я не умею **колоть** дрова.
I can't **chop** firewood.

979 - Мокрый ['mokryj] - *Wet, damp*

Ты оставил ковёр под дождём, и теперь он **мокрый** насквозь.
You've left the carpet under the rain and now it's **wet** through.

980 - Приказ [pri'kaz] - *An order, a command*

Солдаты получили **приказ** наступать.
The soldiers got the **order** to advance.

981 - Прямой [prja'moj] - *Straight*

У него был длинный **прямой** нос и тонкие губы.
He had a long **straight** nose and thin lips.

982 - Закричать [zakri'chat'] - *To cry out (perfective)*

Она хотела **закричать** от радости, но вспомнила что все спят.
She wanted **to cry out** with joy but remembered that everyone was sleeping.

983 - Кончиться ['kontchitsa] - To end; to run out of (perfective)

Это приключение просто не могло **кончиться** хорошо.

That adventure just couldn't **end** well.

984 - Куст [kust] - *A bush*

Мне нравится, как цветёт этот **куст** у моего окна.

I like the way this **bush** by my window blooms.

985 - Стрелять [stre'ljat'] - *To shoot, to fire*

Я не могу **стрелять** в животных.

I can't **shoot** animals.

986 - Художник [hu'dozhnik] - *An artist, a painter*

Этот **художник** скоро открывает новую выставку.

This **artist** is opening a new exhibition soon.

987 - Знак [znak] - *A sign, a mark*

Ты знаешь, для чего используется этот **знак**?

Do you know what this **sign** is used for?

988 - Завод [za'vod] - *A factory, a plant*

Этот **завод** загрязняет окружающую среду.

This **factory** contaminates the environment.

989 - Кулак [ku'lak] - *A fist*

Мальчик сжал **кулак** и погрозил обидчику.

The boy clenched his **fist** and shook it at the offender.

990 - Использовать [is'pol'zavat'] - *To use*

Мы должны эффективно **использовать** эту новую возможность.

We must efficiently **use** this new opportunity

991 - Стакан [sta'kan] - *A glass*

Твой **стакан** наполовину пуст или наполовину полон?
Is your **glass** half empty or half full?

992 - Пахнуть ['pahnut'] - *To smell (of)*

Что может так хорошо **пахнуть**? У меня слюнки текут!
What can **smell** so good? My mouth is watering!

993 - Отсюда [ats'juda'] - *Out of here, from here*

Выведи собаку **отсюда**! Она вся грязная после прогулки.
Get the dog **out of here**! It's all dirty after the walk.

994 - Рот [rot] - *A mouth*

Она открыла **рот**, чтобы возразить, но передумала.
She opened her **mouth** to contradict but changed her mind.

995 - Пора [pa'ra] - *It is time; a season*

Тебе **пора** найти работу и начать жить самостоятельно.
It is time for you to find a job and to start living independently.

996 - Передать [pere'dat'] - *To hand over, to pass*

Я уже стар, и решил **передать** бизнес своим детям.
I'm old and have decided **to hand** the business **over** to my children.

997 - Лечение [le'tchenije] - *Treatment*

Это **лечение** очень дорогое, но эффективное.
This **treatment** is very expensive but very efficient.

998 - Высший ['vysshij] - *The highest*

Она получила **высший** балл за экзамен по математике.
She got **the highest** grade for her Math exam.

999 - Сутки ['sutki] - *24 hours, day and night*

Она заблудилась в лесу и нашла выход только через **сутки**.

She got lost in the woods and found the way out only in 24 hours.

1000 - Вставать [vsta'vat'] - *To stand up, to get up*

Инструктор предупредил нас, что **вставать** в лодке очень опасно.

The instructor warned us that it's very dangerous **to stand up** in a boat.

1001 - Операция [ape'ratsija] - An operation; a surgery; a transaction

Это секретная военная **операция** большой важности.

It's a secret military **operation** of great importance.

1002 - Пространство [prast'ranstvə] - *Space, room*

Каждому члену семьи нужно личное **пространство**.

Every member of the family needs their personal **space**.

1003 - Спокойный [spa'kojnyj] - *Calm, serene*

У этой породы собак **спокойный** и ласковый характер.

This dog breed has a **calm** and tender character.

1004 - Одежда [a'dezhda] - *Clothes, clothing*

Одежда должна быть чистой и аккуратной.

Clothes should be neat and clean.

1005 - Кусок [ku'sok] - *A piece*

Для салата мне нужен большой **кусок** мягкого сыра.

I need a big **piece** of soft cheese for the salad.

1006 - Тема ['tema] - *A subject, a topic*

Тема этого рассказа мне очень близка.

The **subject** of this short story is very close to my heart.

1007 - Животный [zhi'votnyj] - *Animal (adj)*

Животный мир Сибири очень разнообразен.

The **animal** world of Siberia is very diverse.

1008 - Снимать [sni'mat'] - **To take off, to take down; to film**

Пожалуйста, не забывай **снимать** обувь, когда заходишь в дом.

Please, don't forget **to take off** your shoes when you enter the house.

1009 - Искусство [is'kustvə] - *Art*

Настоящее **искусство** понятно всем и не нуждается в объяснениях.

True **art** is clear to everyone and doesn't need any explanations.

1010 - Умный ['umnyj] - **Clever, smart, intelligent**

Он достаточно **умный**, чтобы не обращать внимания на эти сплетни.

He's **clever** enough not to pay attention to this gossip.

1011 - Малый ['malyj] - *Small, little*

Этот закон поддерживает **малый** бизнес.

This law supports **small** business.

1012 - Курс [kurs] - *A course; a policy*

Я подписалась на этот **курс** и ни разу не пожалела об этом.

I signed up for this **course** and I've never regretted it.

1013 - Звонить [zva'nit'] - *To call (by phone); to ring*

Ты можешь **звонить** мне в любое время.
You can **call** me any time.

1014 - Очередной [atchered'noj] - *Next (in order), another*

Очередной этап соревнования состоится через неделю.
The **next** step of the competition will take place in a week.

1015 - Чудо ['tchudə] - *A miracle*

То, что мы выжили в той катастрофе, это настоящее **чудо**.
The fact that we survived that disaster is a real **miracle**.

1016 - Ощущение [astchust'chenije] - *A feeling, a sensation*

Мой дом дарит мне **ощущение** покоя и безопасности.
My house gives me **a feeling** of peace and security.

1017 - Крайне ['krajne] - *Extremely, very (much)*

Сотрудничество с этой компанией стало **крайне** негативным опытом для меня.
The cooperation with that company was an **extremely** negative experience for me.

1018 - Напоминать [napami'nat'] - *To remind; to resemble*

Я не могу всё время **напоминать** тебе о твоих обязанностях!
I can't **remind** you about your duties all the time!

1019 - Придумать [pri'dumat'] - *To figure out; to make up*

Мы должны **придумать**, как подбодрить её.
We must **figure out** how to cheer her up.

1020 - Падать ['padat'] -*To fall; to decline*

Эксперты говорят, что цены будут продолжать **падать**.
Experts say that the prices will go on **falling**.

1021 - Здание ['zdanije] - *A building*

Они планируют снести это старое **здание**.
They're planning to pull down this old **building**.

1022 - Свежий ['svezhij] - *Fresh (new or clean)*

Свежий кофе – это всё, что мне нужно, чтобы проснуться.
Fresh coffee is all I need to wake up.

1023 - Поговорить [pagava'rit'] - *To talk to, to have a conversation; to talk (to have a conversation that lasts a certain period of time; perfective)*

Могу я **поговорить** с вашим начальником?
May I **talk to** your boss?

1024 - Начинаться [natchi'natsa] - *To start, to begin*

Эссе должно **начинаться** со вступления.
An essay should **start** with an introduction.

1025 - Милиция [mi'litsija] - *Militia, police*

Милиция прибыла на место преступления первой.
The **militia** was the first to arrive at the crime scene.

1026 - Приказать [prika'zat'] - *To order, to command*

Я не могу приказать тебе **остаться**, но я был бы очень благодарен.
I can't order you **to stay** but I'd appreciate it a lot.

1027 - Несмотря [nesma'tr'a] - In spite of, despite (always used with preposition 'на')

Несмотря на расстояние, они всегда поддерживают связь.
In spite of the distance they always keep in touch.

1028 - Оттуда [at'tuda] - *From there, out of there*

Давай поднимемся на крышу. **Оттуда** хорошо смотреть на звёзды.
Let's get up to the roof. It's great to watch the stars **from there**.

1029 - Засмеяться [zasme'jatsa] - *To laugh (means to start laughing)*

Я не мог не **засмеяться**, когда услышал твою шутку.
I couldn't help but **laugh** when I heard your joke.

1030 - Волна [val'na] - *A wave, a tide*

Волна была такая огромная, что мы подумали, что это цунами.
The **wave** was so huge that we thought it was a tsunami.

1031 - Задача [za'datcha] - *A task, an assignment*

Эта **задача** требует комплексного подхода.
This **task** demands a comprehensive approach.

1032 - Касаться [ka'satsa] - *To concern; to touch*

Конфликты между родителями не должны **касаться** детей.
The conflicts between parents mustn't **concern** children.

1033 - Старуха [sta'ruha] - *An old woman (colloquial)*

Люди говорили, что **старуха** умеет колдовать.
People used to say that the **old woman** could do witchcraft.

1034 - Войско ['vojskə] - *An army (military), troops*

Повстанцам удалось собрать большое **войско**.

The insurgents managed to gather a great **army**.

1035 - Срок [srok] - *A term; a deadline*

Председатель был избран на пятилетний **срок**.

The chairman was elected for a five-year **term**.

1036 - Ужас ['uzhas] - *Horror, terror*

Невозможно описать **ужас**, который она пережила.

It's impossible to describe the **horror** she experienced.

1037 - Узкий ['uzkij] - *Narrow*

Мне не нравится эта квартира. Коридор слишком **узкий** и комнаты маленькие.

I don't like this apartment. The corridor is too **narrow** and the rooms are small.

1038 - Материал [mater''jal] - *Material, stuff*

Материал, из которого сделаны брюки, очень приятный на ощупь.

The **material** the trousers are made of is very pleasant to touch.

1039 - Приняться [pri'n'atsa] - *To get down to, to start doing*

У вас не так много времени, так что я бы советовал вам **приняться** за дело.

You haven't got much time, so I'd advise you **to get down to** business.

1040 - Нормальный [nar'mal'nyj] - *Normal; sane*

В этой ситуации он повел себя как любой **нормальный** подросток.

In that situation he behaved like any **normal** teenager.

1041 - Крик [krik] - *A cry, a scream*

Её громкий **крик** был слышен даже на втором этаже.

Her loud **cry** was heard even on the second floor.

1042 - Знание ['znanije] - *Knowledge*

Её глубокое **знание** и понимание предмета помогли ей получить повышение.

Her deep **knowledge** and understanding of the subject helped her get a promotion.

1043 - Трое ['troje] - Three (in a group together)

Все **трое** детей простудились после прогулки под дождём.

All the **three** kids caught a cold after the walk in the rain.

1044 - Четвёртый [tchet'vjortyj] - *Fourth*

Это его **четвёртый** гол за сезон.

It's his **fourth** goal in the season.

1045 - Шум [shum] - *A noise*

Шум в квартире соседей мешал мне уснуть.

The **noise** in the neighbors' apartment prevented me from falling asleep.

1046 - Заставить [zas'tavit'] - *To make, to force*

Никто не сможет **заставить** меня изменить моё мнение.

No one will be able **to make** me change my mind.

1047 - Автомат [afto'mat] - A machine gun; a vending machine

Я понятия не имею, как работает **автомат** и чем он отличается от винтовки.

I've got no idea how **a machine gun** works and how it's different from a rifle.

1048 - Резко ['reskə] - Sharply, abruptly, harshly

Она ответила **резко** и грубо.

She answered **sharply** and rudely.

1049 - Тётя ['t'ot'a] - An aunt; a woman (colloquial)

Моя **тётя** часто участвует в волонтерских проектах.

My **aunt** often takes part in volunteer projects.

1050 - Впечатление [fpetchat'lenije] - *An impression*

Невозможно произвести первое **впечатление** дважды.

It's impossible to make the first **impression** twice.

1051 - Пауза ['pauza] - *A pause*

В нашем разговоре возникла долгая неловкая **пауза**.

There was a long and awkward **pause** in our conversation.

1052 - Глубина [glubi'na] - *Depth*

Глубина этой реки не достаточно большая для кораблей.

The **depth** of this river is not big enough for ships.

1053 - Доллар ['dolar] - *A dollar*

Доллар – одна из самых популярных мировых валют.

The dollar is one of the most popular world currencies.

1054 - Сотня ['sotn'a] - *A hundred*

У неё была **сотня** причин расстаться с ним.
She had **a hundred** reasons to break up with him.

1055 - Виноватый [vina'vatyj] - *Guilty*

У собаки был такой **виноватый** вид, что я не мог злиться на неё.
The dog had such a **guilty** look that I couldn't be angry with it.

1056 - Студент [stu'dent] - *A student*

Я **студент**, поэтому я не могу работать на полную ставку.
I am **a student,** which is why I can't work full-time.

1057 - Боевой [baje'voj] - *Battle, combat (adj)*

Дети играли в индейцев и придумали специальный **боевой** клич.
The children were playing Cowboys and Indians and made up a special **battle** cry.

1058 - Очко [atch'ko] - *A point (in a game); blackjack*

Игрок получает одно **очко** за каждый правильный ответ.
A player gets one **point** for every correct answer.

1059 - Нож [nosh] - *A knife*

Этот **нож** слишком тупой, чтобы резать им мясо.
This **knife** is too blunt to cut meat with.

1060 - Подниматься [padni'matsa] - *To rise, to get up*

Уровень воды в реке продолжал **подниматься**, и ситуация становилась опасной.
The level of water in the river was continuing **to rise** and the situation was getting dangerous.

1061 - Мировой [mira'voj] - *World, global, worldwide*

Возможно ли было предвидеть **мировой** финансовый кризис?
Was it possible to foresee the **world** financial crisis?

1062 - Предмет [pred'met] - **An object; a subject, a topic**

При раскопках учёные обнаружили странный **предмет** и сейчас изучают его.
During the excavations the scientists found a strange **object** and are studying it now.

1063 - Плохой [pla'hoj] - *Bad*

Это **плохой** пример. Он ничего не объясняет.
It's a **bad** example. It doesn't explain anything.

1064 - Майор [ma'jor] - *A major (military)*

Старый **майор** выглядел серьёзным и недружелюбным.
The old **major** looked serious and unfriendly.

1065 - Ударить [u'darit'] - *To hit, to strike, to punch*

Если ты не перестанешь, мне придётся тебя **ударить**.
If you don't stop, I'll have **to hit** you.

1066 - Разуметься [razu'metsa] - **Very rarely used in the initial form. Most often used as part of a set expression *'Само собой разумеется'* - 'It goes without saying'.**

Само собой разумеется, что полное выздоровление займёт много времени.
It goes without saying that full recovery will take much time.

1067 - Точный ['tochnyj] - *Exact, precise*

Нам нужен **точный** анализ всех параметров.
We need an **exact** analysis of all the parameters.

1068 - Всякий ['vsjakij] - *Any, every; all sorts of*

Всякий раз, когда я слышу эту песню, я вспоминаю детство.
Anytime I hear this song I recall my childhood.

1069 - Деятельность ['dejatel'nəst'] - *Activity*

Его общественная **деятельность** приносит много пользы другим людям.
His social **activity** does a lot of good to other people.

1070 - Инженер [inzhe'ner] - *An engineer*

Мой дядя – опытный **инженер**, и его часто приглашают протестировать новое оборудование.
My uncle is an experienced **engineer** and he's often invited to test new equipment.

1071 - Программа [prag'rama] - *A program/programme*

Программа обучения состоит из двух частей.
The training **program** consists of two parts.

1072 - Костюм [kast''um] - *A suit; a costume*

Этот **костюм** не подходит мне по размеру.
This **suit** doesn't fit me.

1073 - Женский ['zhenskij] – *Female, feminine, woman's, women's*

Контральто – это тип классического **женского** певческого голоса.
A contralto is a type of classical **female** singing voice.

1074 - Крепкий ['krepkij] - *Tough, strong; firm, solid*

Твой брат **крепкий** парень. Эта работа для него.
Your brother is a **tough** guy. This job is for him.

1075 - Театр [te'atr] - *A theater*

Театр – мой любимый вид искусства.
Theater is my favorite kind of art.

1076 - Встречаться [vstre'chatsa] - *To date; to see each other*

Они начали **встречаться** 3 месяца назад и уже собираются пожениться.
They started **dating** three months ago and they are going to marry already.

1077 - Различный [raz'lichnyj] - *Different; various, diverse*

Мы не можем поместить всех детей в одну группу. У них у всех **различный** уровень подготовленности.
We can't place all the children in one group. They're all at **different** levels of training.

1078 - Хвост [hvost] - *A tail*

У моей кошки длинный пушистый **хвост**.
My cat has a long fluffy **tail**.

1079 - Танк [tank] - *A tank*

Сегодня этот боевой **танк** – музейный экспонат.
Today this battle **tank** is a museum exhibit.

1080 - Социальный [satsi'al'nyj] - *Social*

Этот **социальный** центр поддерживает иммигрантов.
This **social** center supports immigrants.

1081 - Мёртвый ['m'ortvyj] - *Dead; a deadman*

Моя дочь ужасно боится насекомых. Даже **мёртвый** жук может напугать её.

My daughter is terribly scared of insects. Even a **dead** beetle can frighten her.

1082 - Попытаться [papy'tatsa] - *To attempt, to try*

Я хочу хотя бы **попытаться** помириться с ней.

I want at least **to attempt** to make up with her.

1083 - Явно ['javnə] - *Obviously, clearly*

Она **явно** что-то скрывает от нас.

She's **obviously** hiding something from us.

1084 - Журнал [zhur'nal] - *A magazine*

Журнал мод – это единственная книга на её полке.

A fashion **magazine** is the only book on her shelf.

1085 - Конь [kon'] - A horse (a male horse)

Мне кажется, тот чёрный **конь** будет быстрее остальных.

It seems to me that the black **horse** will be faster than the rest.

1086 - Схватить [shva'tit'] - *To grasp, to seize*

Я успел **схватить** мальчика за руку прежде, чем он упал с лестницы.

I managed **to grasp** the boy by the hand before he fell off the ladder.

1087 - Вдоль [vdol'] - *Along*

Мы гуляли **вдоль** реки и разговаривали о прошлом.

We were walking **along** the river and talking about the past.

1088 - Стихи [sti'hi] - *Poems*

Когда я был подростком, я, как и многие другие, пробовал писать **стихи**.

When I was a teenager I, like many others, tried to write **poems**.

1089 - Степень ['stepen'] - *An extent, a degree*

Степень участия в проекте может быть разной. Главное, чтобы все внесли свой вклад.

The **extent** of participation in the project may be different. The main thing is that everyone adds value.

1090 - Отказаться [atka'zatsa] - *To refuse; to give up*

Я не в настроении ехать на экскурсию. Могу я **отказаться**?

I'm not in the mood to go on excursion. Can I **refuse**?

1091 - Вытащить ['vytastchit'] - *To pull out, to drag out*

Мне пришлось схватить щенка за уши, чтобы **вытащить** его из воды.

I had to grasp the puppy by the ears to **pull** it **out of** water.

1092 - Предлагать [predla'gat'] - *To offer; to suggest*

Наша компания планирует **предлагать** услуги маркетинга.

Our company is planning **to offer** marketing services.

1093 - Фигура [fi'gura] - *A figure*

У тебя идеальная **фигура**. Что ты делаешь, чтобы держать себя в форме?

You've got a perfect **figure**. What do you do to keep in shape?

1094 - Ключ [kl'utch] - *A key*

Я потерял **ключ** от входной двери, и мне пришлось заменить замок.

I've lost the **key** to the front door and had to replace the lock.

1095 - Чёрт [tchort] - Devil (very often used in set expressions like 'Чёрт с тобой!' - "To hell with you!")

Он такой хитрый, что, похоже, даже сам **чёрт** не сможет его обмануть.

He's so cunning that, apparently, even the **devil** himself won't be able to deceive him.

1096 - Отправиться [at'pravitsa] - To go on, to go to; to set off (perfective)

Я хотел **отправиться** в круиз, но мне пришлось всё отменить из-за болезни отца.

I wanted **to go on** a cruise but I had to cancel everything because of my father's illness.

1097 - Побежать [pabe'zhat'] - *To start running*

Она хотела **побежать** за автобусом, но поняла, что всё равно не догонит его.

She wanted **to start running** after the bus but realized she would not catch up with it anyway.

1098 - Вагон [va'gon] - *A car (on a train)*

Спальный **вагон** был душным и неудобным.

The sleeping **car** was stuffy and uncomfortable.

1099 - Культура [kul'tura] - *Culture*

Культура каждой нации по-своему уникальна.

The **culture** of every nation is unique in its own way.

1100 - Курить [ku'rit'] - *To smoke*

Ты должен бросить **курить**, иначе тебя не примут в команду.
You must give up **smoking**, otherwise they won't accept you in the team.

1101 - Боец [ba'jets] - *A fighter; a soldier*

Это маленькая девочка настоящий **боец**. У неё было три операции!
This little girl is a real **fighter.** She has had three surgeries!

1102 - Западный ['zapadnyj] - *Western*

Западный мир никогда не поймёт восточный и наоборот.
The **Western** world will never understand the Eastern one and vice versa.

1103 - Фильм [fil'm] - *A film, a movie*

Этот исторический **фильм** вдохновил меня на написание новой статьи.
This historical **film** inspired me to write a new article.

1104 - Восемь ['vosem'] - *Eight*

В этом классе всего **восемь** учеников.
There are only **eight** pupils in this class.

1105 - Открывать [atkry'vat'] - *To open*

Я прошу тебя не **открывать** подарки до твоего дня рождения.
I ask you not **to open** the presents before your birthday.

1106 - Зайти [zaj'ti] - *To drop by (perfective)*

Я хочу поговорить с тобой. Можно мне **зайти** после работы?
I want to talk to you. May I **drop by** after work?

1107 - Немедленно [ne'medlennə] - *Immediately*

Вы должны **немедленно** отвезти ребёнка в больницу!
You must **immediately** take the child to the hospital!

1108 - Замечать [zame'tchat'] - *To notice, to note*

Теперь я начинаю **замечать**, что ты сильно изменился.
Now I'm beginning **to notice** that you've changed a lot.

1109 - Пыль [pyl'] - *Dust*

Нам придётся долго убирать этот старый дом. **Пыль** повсюду!
We'll have to clean this old house for a long time. **Dust** is everywhere!

1110 - Закончить [za'kontchit'] - *To finish, to end (perfective)*

Мне нужно ещё немного времени, чтобы **закончить** книгу.
I need some more time **to finish** the book.

1111 - Мягкий ['mjahkij] - *Soft; mild*

Какой **мягкий** пирог! Он просто тает во рту!
What a **soft** cake! It's just melting in the mouth!

1112 - Труба [tru'ba] - *A pipe, a tube; a trumpet*

Я только что заметил, что эта **труба** протекает. Мы должны вызвать сантехника.
I've just noticed that this **pipe** is leaking. We must call a plumber.

1113 - Редкий ['redkij] - *Rare*

Это **редкий** вид бабочек. Он занесён в Красную книгу.
It's a **rare** species of butterfly. It's listed in the Red Book.

1114 - Миллион [mili'on] - *A million*

Что бы ты делал, если бы выиграл **миллион** долларов?
What would you do if you won **a million** dollars?

1115 - Следить [sled"it'] - *To follow, to watch; to spy*

Мы будем **следить** за событиями на соревнованиях.
We are going **to follow** the events at the competitions.

1116 - Масса ['masa] - *Mass (weight); mass (a lot of)*

Какова точная **масса** этой машины? Наше оборудование сможет поднять её?
What's the exact **weight** of this car? Will our equipment be able to lift it?

1117 - Пятьдесят [p'at'de's'at] - *Fifty*

Ты читала "**Пятьдесят** оттенков серого"?
Have you read "The **Fifty** Shades of Grey"?

1118 - Обстоятельство [absta'jatel'stvə] - *A circumstance*

Это **обстоятельство** помешало нам закончить проект раньше.
That **circumstance** prevented us from finishing the project earlier.

1119 - Решиться [re'shitsa] - *To dare*

Она не могла **решиться** рассказать нам правду, боясь, что мы не поймём её.
She couldn't **dare** to tell us the truth because she was afraid we wouldn't understand her.

1120 - Одновременно [adnavre'mennə] - *Simultaneously*

Я слышал несколько голосов **одновременно**.
I could hear a few voices **simultaneously**.

1121 - Броситься ['brositsa] - *To rush, to dash*

Мне хотелось **броситься** к ней и обнять её.
I wanted **to rush** to her and embrace her.

1122 - Пошлый ['poshlyj] - *Vulgar*

Его **пошлый** анекдот смутил девушку.
His **vulgar** joke embarrassed the girl.

1123 - Круглый ['kruglyj] - *Round (adj)*

Посреди комнаты стоит маленький **круглый** стол.
There's a small **round** table standing in the middle of the room.

1124 - Штаб [shtab] - *A headquarters (military)*

Штаб фронта был расположен на севере страны.
The **headquarters** of the front was situated in the North of the country.

1125 - Слух [sluh] - *Hearing; a rumor*

Слух может ухудшаться с возрастом.
Hearing can get worse with age.

1126 - Голый ['golyj] - *Bare, naked, nude*

В комнате не было даже ковра, только **голый** пол.
There wasn't a carpet in the room, only **bare** floor.

1127 - Закрыть [zak'ryt'] - To close, to shut (perfective)

Можешь **закрыть** окно? Холодно.
Can you **close** the window? It's cold.

1128 - Линия ['linija] - *A line*

Красная **линия** разделила страницу на две части.
A red **line** divided the page into two parts.

1129 - Лодка ['lodka] - *A boat*

Это **лодка** моего дедушки. Он на ней рыбачит.
It's my granddad's **boat**. He goes fishing on it.

1130 - Наоборот [naaba'rot] - Vice versa, the other way round

Это ты должен извиняться передо мной, а не **наоборот**.
It's you who should apologize to me and not **vice versa**.

1131 - Даль [dal'] - *Distance, far*

Она задумчиво смотрела в недостижимую **даль**.
She was looking into the **distance** thoughtfully.

1132 - Председатель [predse'datel'] - *A chairman*

Председатель комитета предложил начать голосование.
The **chairman** of the committee suggested to start the vote.

1133 - Понравиться [pan'ravitsa] - To like (the person who likes takes the dative case) (perfective)

Эта книга должна тебе **понравиться**. Это новый детектив.
You must **like** this book. It's a new detective story.

1134 - Обратиться [abra'titsa] - *To turn to, to address (perfective)*

Тебе нужно **обратиться** к специалисту. Это слишком сложный вопрос.

You should **turn to** a specialist. This matter is too complicated.

1135 - Период [pe'riəd] - *A period; an epoch*

Это был сложный **период** их отношений, но они смогли сохранить их.

That was a hard **period** of their relationship but they managed to save it.

1136 - Организм [arga'nism] - *An organism, a body*

Человеческий **организм** – это удивительный механизм.

The human **organism** is an amazing mechanism.

1137 - Отдел [at'del] - *A department*

Отдел продаж находится в другом здании.

The sales **department** is in a different building.

1138 - Весна [ves'na] - *Spring*

Ранняя **весна** обычно холодная и дождливая.

Early **spring** is usually cold and rainy.

1139 - Обед [a'bed] - *Dinner, lunch*

Что у нас на **обед**? Я умираю от голода!

What have we got for **dinner**? I'm starving!

1140 - Значение [zna'tchenije] - *A meaning*

У этого слова есть ещё одно **значение**.

This word has one more **meaning**.

1141 - Дно [dno] - *Bottom*

Дно океана – это загадочное место.
The **bottom** of the ocean is a mysterious place.

1142 - Фотография [fota'grafija] - *A photo*

Эта семейная **фотография** мне очень дорога.
This family **photo** is very dear to me.

1143 - Некий ['nekij] - *Some, a certain*

Некий господин Иванов хочет видеть Вас.
Some Mr. Ivanov wants to see you.

1144 - Успех [us'peh] - *Success*

Успех проекта зависит от качества сотрудничества.
The **success** of the project depends on the quality of collaboration.

1145 - Грязный ['grjaznyj] - *Dirty, muddy*

Почему ковёр такой **грязный**? Мне придётся отдать его в химчистку.
Why is the carpet so **dirty**? I'll have to take it to the dry-cleaner's.

1146 - Естественный [jes'testvennyj] - *Natural*

Это твой **естественный** цвет волос?
Is it your **natural** hair color?

1147 - Велеть [ve'let'] - *To order, to command (literary, archaic)*

Если хочешь, я могу **велеть** ей вернуть твои вещи.
If you want, I can **order** her to give your things back.

1148 - Сцена ['stsena] - *A stage; a scene*

Сцена – это её жизнь. Она отличная актриса.
The **stage** is her life. She's an excellent actress.

1149 - Билет [bi'let] - *A ticket*

У меня есть свободный **билет** на матч. Пойдёшь со мной?
I have a spare **ticket** to the match. Are you going with me?

1150 - Состав [sas'tav] - *Content, composition*

Я всегда обращаю внимание на **состав** продуктов питания.
I always pay attention to the **content** of foods.

1151 - Знаменитый [zname'nityj] - *Famous*

Знаменитый пианист даёт сегодня концерт в нашем городе.
Today a **famous** pianist is giving a concert in our city.

1152 - Лишний ['lishnyj] - *Extra; superfluous, excess*

Я знала, что ты придёшь, и подготовила **лишний** стул.
I knew you'd come and prepared an **extra** chair.

1153 - Честь [tchest'] - *Honor*

Эта улица названа в **честь** героя войны.
This street is named in **honor** of a war hero.

1154 - Иметься [i'metsa] - *There be, there is/are, to be, to be available*

В любом городе должна **иметься** хотя бы одна больница.
There should **be** at least one hospital in any town.

1155 - Смех [smeh] - *Laughter, laugh*

В парке развлечений детский **смех** был слышен повсюду.
In the amusement park children's **laughter** was heard everywhere.

1156 - СССР [ɛs ɛs ɛs 'ɛr] - *USSR*

СССР был антирелигиозным государством.
USSR was an anti-religious state.

1157 - Деревянный [dere'vjannyj] - *Wooden*

Наш дачный домик **деревянный**, поэтому летом в нём прохладно.

Our country house is **wooden**, which is why in summer it's cool inside.

1158 - Опустить [apus'tit'] - *To put down; to omit*

Полицейский приказал грабителю **опустить** пистолет.

The policeman ordered the robber **to put down** the gun.

1159 - Родиться [ra'ditsa] - *To be born*

Я бы хотел **родиться** в другую эпоху.

I wish I **were born** in a different epoch.

1160 - Способ ['sposəb] - *A means, a way*

Интернет – самый популярный **способ** общения среди молодежи.

The Internet is the most popular **means** of communication among the youth.

1161 - Спасти [spas'ti] - *To save, to rescue*

Им удалось **спасти** альпиниста только через три дня.

They managed **to save** the climber in only three days.

1162 - Зрение ['zrenije] - *Eyesight, vision*

У неё очень плохое **зрение**. Она ничего не видит без очков.

She's got very poor **eyesight**. She doesn't see anything without glasses.

1163 - Английский [an'glijskij] - *English*

Английский язык самый популярный из всех мировых языков.

The **English** language is the most popular among the world languages.

1164 - Отдельный [at'del'nyj] - *Separate, detached; individual*

У этой комнаты есть **отдельный** вход.
This room has a **separate** entrance.

1165 - Извинить [izvi'nit'] - **To excuse, to pardon, to forgive (for)**

Вам придётся **извинить** меня, но мне пора идти. Спасибо за отличный вечер!
You'll have **to excuse** me but it's time for me to go. Thank you for the great night!

1166 - Громкий ['gromkij] - *Loud*

Меня разбудил **громкий** раскат грозы.
I was woken up by a **loud** peal of thunder.

1167 - Объявить [abja'vit'] - *To announce, to declare*

Мы решили **объявить** о помолвке.
We've decided **to announce** the engagement.

1168 - Запад ['zapad] - *West*

Запад страны более развит экономически.
The **west** of the country is more developed economically.

1169 - Германия [ger'manija] - *Germany*

Германия уделяет большое внимание проблемам окружающей среды.
Germany pays great attention to the problems of the environment.

1170 - Обращаться [abra'stchatsa] - *To turn to, to address*

Я не люблю **обращаться** к врачам за помощью и редко хожу в больницу.
I don't like **to turn to** doctors for help and rarely go to hospital.

1171 - Население [nase'lenije] - *Population*

Население страны растёт недостаточно быстро.
The **population** of the country doesn't grow fast enough.

1172 - Беда [be'da] - **A trouble, a misfortune**

Та страшная **беда** навсегда изменила его жизнь.
That terrible **trouble** changed his life forever.

1173 - Спешить [spe'shit'] - *To hurry, to be in a hurry*

Нам нужно **спешить**. Такси уже ждёт.
We need **to hurry**. The taxi is waiting already.

1174 - Еда [je'da] - *Food; a meal*

Здоровая **еда** – это ключ к долгой жизни.
Healthy **food** is the key to a long life.

1175 - Поздно ['poznə] - *Late*

Уже **поздно**. Детям пора ложиться спать.
It's **late** already. It's time for the kids to go to bed.

1176 - Специальный [spetsi'alnyj] - *Special, custom*

Я выиграл **специальный** приз конкурса.
I won the **special** prize of the contest.

1177 - Наблюдать [nabl'u'dat'] - *To watch, to observe*

Я люблю **наблюдать** за птицами. Они удивительные создания.
I like **to watch** birds. They're amazing creatures.

1178 - Еврей [ev'rej] - *A Jew, a Hebrew*

Этот пожилой **еврей** – очень хороший ювелир.
This elderly **Jew** is a very good goldsmith.

1179 - Ой [oj] - *Oh, oops, auch*

Ой, я наступила тебе на ногу. Я не нарочно.
Oh, I've stepped on your foot. That wasn't on purpose.

1180 - Суметь [su'met'] - *To be able, to manage, to succeed*

Ты должен **суметь** убедить её поехать с нами.
You must **be able to** persuade her to go with us.

1181 - Обернуться [aber'nutsa] - *To turn around; to result in*

Не успел я **обернуться**, как собака схватила мой бутерброд и выбежала из комнаты.
Hardly had I managed **to turn around** when the dog seized my sandwich and ran out of the room.

1182 - Министр [mi'nistr] - *A minister*

Министр иностранных дел прибыл с официальным визитом.
The **Minister** of Foreign Affairs arrived on an official visit.

1183 - Фирма ['firma] - *A firm, a company*

Их **фирма** обанкротилась во время кризиса.
Their **firm** went bankrupt during the crisis.

1184 - Проснуться [pras'nutsa] - *To wake up (perfective)*

Я не могу **проснуться** без чашки крепкого кофе.
I can't **wake up** without a cup of strong coffee.

1185 - Организация [argani'zatsija] - *An organisation*

ООН – это влиятельная международная **организация**.
The UN is an influential international **organization**.

1186 - Принцип ['printsip] - *A principle*

Я не могу понять **принцип** работы этого механизма.
I can't understand the **principle** of work of this mechanism.

1187 - Направление [naprav'lenije] - *A direction*

Я думаю, мы выбрали правильное **направление** развития.
I think we've chosen the right **direction** of development.

1188 - Гораздо [ga'razdə] - *Much, far, by far*

Мне кажется, что книга **гораздо** интереснее фильма.
It seems to me that the book is **much** more interesting than the movie.

1189 - Мастер ['master] - *A master, an expert*

Этот ремесленник – настоящий **мастер**. Его работы уникальны.
This craftsman is a real **master**. His works are unique.

1190 - Подождать [padazh'dat'] - *To wait (perfective)*

Ваши фотографии ещё не готовы. Вам придётся **подождать**.
Your photos are not ready yet. You'll have **to wait**.

1191 - Светлый ['svetlyj] - *Light (shade)*

Я выбираю этот **светлый** плащ. Тёмный мне не подходит.
I choose this **light** raincoat. The dark one doesn't suit me.

1192 - Ошибка [a'shibka] - *A mistake*

Эта **ошибка** испортила весь результат.
This **mistake** ruined the whole result.

1193 - Высота [vysa'ta] - *Height*

Высота этого небоскрёба просто поражает.
The **height** of this skyscraper is just stunning.

1194 - Существо [sustchest'vo] - *A creature*

Синий кит – самое большое **существо** на планете.
The blue whale is the biggest **creature** on the planet.

1195 - Заговорить [zagava'rit'] - *To begin to talk*

Он не мог осмелиться даже **заговорить** с ней.
He couldn't dare even **to begin talking with** her.

1196 - Мальчишка [mal''tchishka] - *A boy, a kid, a brat*

Ты просто избалованный **мальчишка**!
You're just a spoiled **boy**!

1197 - Пользоваться ['pol'zavatsa] - *To use; to enjoy (success for example)*

Ты можешь **пользоваться** любыми вещами, которые тебе нужны. Чувствуй себя как дома.
You can **use** anything you need. Make yourself at home.

1198 - Научный ['nautchnyj] - *Scientific*

Давай попробуем применить **научный** подход.
Let's try to apply a **scientific** approach.

1199 - Повторять [pavta'rjat'] - *To repeat; to revise*

При изучении иностранного языка очень полезно **повторять** каждое слово вслух.
It's very useful **to repeat** each word aloud when learning a foreign language.

1200 - Яркий ['jarkij] - *Bright*

Мне нравится **яркий** узор на твоей майке.
I like the **bright** pattern on your T-shirt.

1201 - Несколько ['neskal'ka] - *A few, some*

У меня есть **несколько** вопросов. Вы можете уделить мне немного времени?

I've got **a few** questions. Can you devote some time to me?

1202 - Учить [u'tchit'] - *To learn, to study; to teach*

Я не могу **учить** новые слова, не записывая их.

I can't **learn** new words without writing them down.

1203 - Взяться ['vzjatsa] - *To undertake*

Я не смогу **взяться** за новый проект, пока не закончу этот.

I won't be able **to undertake** a new project until I finish this one.

1204 - Бегать ['begat'] - *To run*

Пожалуйста, перестань **бегать** по дому и успокойся.

Please, stop **running** about the house and calm down.

1205 - Господь [gas'pod'] - *Lord, God*

Господь милостив! Он поможет!

Lord is merciful! He'll help!

1206 - Общественный [abst'chestvennyj] - *Public, common; social*

Я трачу довольно много денег на **общественный** транспорт.

I spend quite a lot of money on **public** transport.

1207 - Устроить [ust'roit'] - *To arrange, to organize*

Хотите комнату с видом на море? Я могу это **устроить**.

Do you want a room with a sea view? I can **arrange** that.

1208 - Дышать [dy'shat'] - *To breathe*

Хочу жить там, где смогу **дышать** чистым воздухом.

I want to live where I can **breathe** clean air.

1209 - Лечь [letch'] - *To lie down*

Тебе лучше **лечь** и оставаться в постели некоторое время.
You'd better **lie down** and stay in bed for some time.

1210 - США [sɛ shɛ 'a] - *The USA*

США расположены между Мексикой и Канадой.
The USA is situated between Mexico and Canada.

1211 - Камера ['kamera] - A camera (photography); a chamber; a cell (in prison)

Мне нужна новая **камера**, чтобы делать фотографии более высокого качества.
I need a new **camera** to take photos of a better quality.

1212 - Победа [pa'beda] - *Victory*

Победа в чемпионате сделала его всемирно знаменитым.
The **victory** in the championship made him world famous.

1213 - Учёный [u'tchjonyj] - *Learned, academic*

Мой **учёный** друг лучше энциклопедии, но он такой рассеянный!
My **learned** friend is better than an encyclopedia but he's so absent-minded!

1214 - Состоять [sasta'jat'] - To consist (of); to be a member of

Экзамен будет **состоять** из трёх частей, включая практическое задание.
The exam will **consist of** three parts including the practical task.

1215 - Заходить [zaha'dit'] - To enter, to come in (to); to drop by

Я не разрешаю **заходить** в мою комнату без стука.

I don't allow anyone **to enter** my room without knocking.

1216 - Человечество [tchela'vetchestvə] - *Mankind, humankind, humanity*

Сегодня **человечество** утратило многие традиционные ценности.

Today **mankind** has lost many traditional values.

1217 - Фраза ['fraza] - *A phrase*

Его **фраза** прозвучала очень грубо.

His **phrase** sounded very rude.

1218 - Внимательно [vni'matel'nə] - *Attentively*

Постарайтесь слушать **внимательно**. Я не буду повторять дважды.

Try to listen **attentively**. I won't repeat twice.

1219 - Считаться [stchi'tatsa] - *To be considered (impersonal)*

Как такое поведение может **считаться** нормальным?

How can such behavior **be considered** normal?

1220 - Вероятно [vera'jatnə] - *Probably, very likely*

Вы, **вероятно**, ещё не слышали последние новости.

You **probably** haven't heard the latest news yet.

1221 - Соседний [sa'sednij] - *Neighboring, next to*

Соседний дом продаётся. Ты не знаешь, сколько они хотят за него?

The **neighboring** house is for sale. Do you know how much they want for it?

1222 - Замок [za'mok] - *A lock*

На этом сейфе кодовый **замок**. Его очень сложно открыть.
There's a coded **lock** on this safe. It's very hard to open.

1223 - Рыжий ['ryzhyj] - *Red, ginger (of hair)*

Мой толстый **рыжий** кот такой ленивый! Он даже не знает, как ловить мышей.
My fat **ginger** cat is so lazy! He doesn't even know how to catch mice.

1224 - Ездить ['jezdit'] - To go (by horse or vehicle), to ride, to drive

Он любит **ездить** в экзотические страны. Он уже посетил больше десятка.
He likes **going** to exotic countries. He's already visited more than a dozen.

1225 - Господи ['gospadi] - *Lord, God (as a vocative)*

О, **Господи**! Что же мы теперь будем делать?
Oh, **Lord**! What are we going to do now?

1226 - Остановить [astana'vit'] - *To stop (perfective)*

Нужно делать всё возможное, чтобы **остановить** глобальное потепление.
We should do everything possible **to stop** the global warming.

1227 - Встретиться ['vstretitsa] - *To meet (with); to come across*

Я хочу **встретиться** с ней и обсудить детали контракта.
I want **to meet** with her and discuss the details of the contract.

1228 - Явиться [ja'vitsa] - *To show up, to turn up*

Послушай, ты не можешь **явиться** на собеседование в шортах.
Listen, you can't **show up** to a job interview in shorts.

1229 - Рынок ['rynək] - **A marketplace; a market**

Давай сходим на **рынок** в субботу. Я хочу купить свежей рыбы к празднику.
Let's go to the **marketplace** on Saturday. I want to buy some fresh fish for the holiday.

1230 - Тяжело [tjazhe'lo] - *Hard, difficultly; heavily*

Тяжело совмещать семью и карьеру.
It's **hard** to combine a family and a career.

1231 - Злой [zloj] - *Evil, mean*

Злой волшебник жил глубоко в лесу.
The **evil** magician lived deep in the woods.

1232 - Клуб [klub] - *A club*

В нашем районе открылся новый ночной **клуб**.
They've opened a new night **club** in our district.

1233 - Привезти [prives'ti] - *To bring (by vehicle)*

Эти строительные материалы слишком тяжёлые. Мы не сможем **привезти** их на своей машине.
These building materials are too heavy. We won't be able to **bring** them in our car.

1234 - Платить [pla'tit'] - *To pay*

Жители города отказались **платить** новый налог.
The citizens refused **to pay** the new tax.

1235 - Кость [kost'] - *A bone*

Рентген показал, что **кость** сломана.

The X-ray showed that the **bone** was broken.

1236 - Дикий ['dikij] - *Wild*

Этот волк – **дикий** зверь. Я не думаю, что ты сможешь приручить его.

This wolf is a **wild** beast. I don't think you'll be able to tame it.

1237 - Личность ['lichnəst'] - *Personality; a person, an individual*

Он действительно уникальная **личность**. Я раньше никогда не встречал таких людей.

He's got a really unique **personality**. I've never met such people before.

1238 - Столица [sta'litsa] - *A capital*

Любая **столица** – это центр культурной и политической жизни страны.

Any **capital** is the center of cultural and political life of the country.

1239 - Спасть [spast'] - *To break, to fall (to decrease)*

Прогноз погоды говорит, что жара должна **спасть** к концу месяца.

The weather forecast says that the heat should **break** by the end of the month.

1240 - Здоровье [zda'rovje] - *Health*

Моё **здоровье** заметно улучшилось по сравнению с прошлым годом.

My **health** has improved notably in comparison with the previous year.

1241 - Здравствовать ['zdrastvəvat'] - *To prosper, to thrive*

Мы надеемся, что вы будете **здравствовать** ещё долгие годы!
We hope you'll **prosper** for many years to come!

1242 - Попытка [pa'pytka] - *A try, an attempt*

Хорошая **попытка**! Но ты опять не угадал.
A nice **try**! But you haven't guessed it again.

1243 - Позволять [pazva'ljat'] - *To allow, to permit*

Как ты можешь **позволять** своим детям так с тобой разговаривать?
How can you **allow** your children to talk to you like that?

1244 - Наиболее [nai'boleje] - *The most, most of all*

Это **наиболее** эффективный метод лечения.
It's **the most** efficient method of treatment.

1245 - Постепенно [paste'pennə] - *Gradually, step by step*

Изменения будут внедряться **постепенно**.
The changes are going to be implemented **gradually**.

1246 - Пятый ['pjatyj] - *Fifth*

Май – это **пятый** месяц года.
May is the **fifth** month of the year.

1247 - Определённый [aprede'ljonnyj] - *Certain, definite*

В **определённый** момент мы просто перестали общаться.
At a **certain** moment we just stopped communicating.

1248 - Читатель [tchi'tatel'] - *A reader*

Дорогой **читатель**, эта книга полна приключений.
Dear **reader**, this book is full of adventures.

1249 - Шутка ['shutka] - *A joke*

Шутка была такая смешная, что мы катались от смеха.
The **joke** was so funny that we were rolling with laughter.

1250 - Исторический [ista'ritcheskij] - *Historical; historic*

Исторический центр города привлекает много туристов.
The **historical** center of the city attracts lots of tourists.

1251 - Вслед [vsled] - **After, behind, following**

Она с грустью смотрела **вслед** уходящему поезду.
She was looking **after** the leaving train with sadness.

1252 - Сотрудник [sat'rudnik] - *An employee*

Каждый **сотрудник** компании получил подарок к Рождеству.
Every **employee** of the company got a present for Christmas.

1253 - Внутри [vnut'ri] - *Inside*

Не открывай коробку! Ты не знаешь, что **внутри**.
Don't open the box! You don't know what's **inside**.

1254 - Собственно ['sobstvennə] - **Actually, as a matter of fact, in fact**

Я, **собственно**, не собираюсь оставаться здесь навсегда.
Actually, I'm not going to stay here forever.

1255 - Родина ['rodina] - *Motherland*

Моя **родина** находится далеко отсюда, и я очень по ней скучаю.
My **motherland** is far away from here and I miss it a lot.

1256 - Царь [tsar'] - *Tsar*

Николай II – это последний русский **царь**.

Nicolas II is the last Russian **tsar**.

1257 - Насчёт [nas'tchjot] - **About, concerning (colloquial)**

Как **насчёт** сходить завтра в кафе?

What **about** going to the cafe tomorrow?

1258 - Страница [stra'nitsa] - *A page*

Похоже, это **страница** из твоего дневника.

Looks like it's **a page** from your diary.

1259 - Скорость ['skorast'] - *Speed*

Какова максимальная **скорость** этого автомобиля?

What's the maximum **speed** of this car?

1260 - Зверь [zver'] - **An animal, a beast; a brute (figurative)**

Этот белый медведь выглядит милым, но это дикий и опасный **зверь**.

This polar bear looks cute but it's a wild and dangerous **animal**.

1261 - Помочь [pa'motch] - *To help (perfective)*

Я смогу **помочь** только после обеда. Пойдёт?

I'll be able **to help** only in the afternoon. Will it do?

1262 - Заявить [zaja'vit'] - **To declare, to state, to claim**

Он был достаточно смелым, чтобы открыто **заявить** о своём недовольстве властями.

He was bold enough to openly **declare** his dissatisfaction with the authorities.

1263 - Нечто ['netchtə] - Something; awesome (colloquial)

Нечто странное и большое шевелилось в темноте.
Something big and strange was moving in the darkness.

1264 - Размер [raz'mer] - *A size*

Тебе не кажется, что мне нужен **размер** побольше?
Doesn't it seem to you that I need a bigger **size**?

1265 - Житель ['zhitel'] - *An inhabitant, a resident*

Этот пожилой человек – местный **житель** острова.
This elderly man is a local **inhabitant** of the island.

1266 - Секретарь [sekre'tar'] - *A secretary*

Мне нужен опытный **секретарь** со знанием иностранных языков.
I need an experienced **secretary** with the knowledge of foreign languages.

1267 - Городской [garats'koj] - *Urban; town, city (adj)*

Городской темп жизни не для меня.
The **urban** pace of life is not for me.

1268 - Прекрасно [prek'rasnə] - *Beautifully, nice, great*

Ваша дочь **прекрасно** поёт. Кем она хочет стать в будущем?
Your daughter sings **beautifully**. What does she want to be in the future?

1269 - Торчать [tar'chat'] - To stick out; to hang around (colloquial)

Старайся выглядеть опрятно. Рубашка не должна вот так вот **торчать** из брюк.
Try to look neat. The shirt shouldn't **stick out** of your trousers like this.

1270 - Многое ['mnogaje] - *Many things, much*

Я **многое** понял после того, как стал родителем.
I realized **many things** after I became a parent.

1271 - Америка [a'merica] - *America*

Америка была названа в честь Америго Веспуччи.
America was named in honor of Amerigo Vespucci.

1272 - Сигарета [siga'reta] - *A cigarette*

У тебя осталась только одна **сигарета**. Может, пора бросать курить?
You've got only one **cigarette** left. Maybe it's time to give up smoking?

1273 - Полностью ['polnastju] - *Completely, entirely, fully*

Я **полностью** согласна с твоим мнением.
I **completely** agree with your opinion.

1274 - Пиво ['pivə] - *Beer*

Я не люблю **пиво**. Оно для меня слишком горькое на вкус.
I don't like **beer**. It tastes too bitter to me.

1275 - Приём [pri'jom] - *A reception; an appointment (very often at the doctor's)*

Это был роскошный **приём**! Я под впечатлением!
That was a luxurious **reception**! I'm impressed!

1276 - Противник [pra'tivnik] - *An opponent; an enemy*

Наш **противник** очень опытный, но я думаю, что мы выиграем завтрашний матч.
Our **opponent** is very experienced, but I think we'll win tomorrow's match.

1277 - Образование [abrazo'vanije] - *Education*

Сегодня мы считаем **образование** необходимостью, а не роскошью.

Today we consider **education** to be a necessity, not a luxury.

1278 - Продукт [pra'duct] - **A product (commodity for sale); a food stuff**

Сейчас наша команда тестирует новый **продукт**.

Our team is testing a new **product** now.

1279 - Поймать [paj'mat'] - **To catch (both literally and figuratively)**

Я надеюсь **поймать** такси и вернуться домой до полуночи.

I hope **to catch** a taxi and to return home before midnight.

1280 - Пуля ['pulja] - *A bullet*

К счастью, это была не настоящая **пуля**, а резиновая.

Luckily, that wasn't a real **bullet** but a rubber one.

1281 - Книжка ['knizhka] - **A book (more colloquial variant of 'книга')**

Это не моя **книжка**. Я взял её в библиотеке.

It's not my **book**. I borrowed it from the library.

1282 - Дальний ['dal'nij] - *Far, distant, remote*

Его отправили в командировку на **Дальний** Восток.

He was sent on a business trip to the **Far** East.

1283 - Экономический [ɛkana'mitcheskij] - *Economic, economical*

В следующем году наша страна примет международный **экономический** форум.

Next year our country is hosting an international **economic** forum.

1284 - Представитель [predsta'vitel'] - *A representative*

Представитель нашей партии не смог присутствовать на собрании.

The **representative** of our party was unable to be present at the meeting.

1285 - Собирать [sabi'rat'] - *To gather, to collect, to harvest*

Это приложение помогает **собирать** информацию потребителей.

This application helps **to gather** consumers' information.

1286 - Видимый ['vidimyj] - *Visible*

Нам нужен **видимый** результат, а не бесконечные обещания.

We need a **visible** result and not endless promises.

1287 - Производство [praiz'vodstvə] - *Production, manufacture*

Страна расширяет **производство** натуральных продуктов.

The country is expanding the **production** of natural foods.

1288 - Больница [bal'nitsa] - *A hospital*

Местная **больница** испытывает недостаток врачей.

The local **hospital** is experiencing a lack of doctors.

1289 - Ресторан [resta'ran] - *A restaurant*

Этот **ресторан** знаменит своим шеф-поваром.

This **restaurant** is famous for its chef.

1290 - Находить [naha'dit'] - *To find; to consider, to think*

Студенты должны уметь **находить** информацию самостоятельно.

Students must be able **to find** information independently.

1291 - Диван [di'van] - *A sofa, a couch*

Садись на **диван**. Он мягче, чем стулья.
Sit down on the **sofa**. It's softer than the chairs.

1292 - Дыхание [dy'hanije] - *Breathing; breath*

Тяжёлое **дыхание** пациента волновало врача.
The patient's heavy **breathing** troubled the doctor.

1293 - Тюрьма [tjur'ma] - *A prison*

Это **тюрьма** для несовершеннолетних преступников.
This **prison** is for underage criminals.

1294 - Лёгкое ['ljohkəje] - *A lung*

Врачам пришлось удалить ей одно **лёгкое**, чтобы спасти ей жизнь.
The doctors had to remove one **lung** of hers to save her life.

1295 - Мясо ['m'asə] - *Meat*

Я вегетарианец. Я не ем **мясо** уже более десяти лет.
I'm a vegetarian. I haven't been eating any **meat** for more than ten years already.

1296 - Внизу [vni'zu] - **Below, underneath; at the foot of**

Внизу есть список необходимых документов.
There's a list of necessary documents **below**.

1297 - Кошка ['koshka] - *A cat (female)*

Наша **кошка** родила четыре милых котёнка.
Our **cat** gave birth to four cute kittens.

1298 - Взрослый ['vzroslyj] - Grown-up; a grown-up, an adult;

Ты уже **взрослый** человек и должен уметь заботиться о себе.
You are a **grown-up** person already and must be able to take care of yourself.

1299 - Отсутствие [at'sutstvije] - *Absence*

Отсутствие чётких инструкций привело к недопониманию.
The **absence** of clear instructions led to misunderstanding.

1300 - Настроение [nastra'jenije] - *Mood*

Сегодня мой день рождения и у меня отличное **настроение**!
Today is my birthday and I'm in a great **mood**!

1301 - Собрать [sab'rat'] - To gather, to collect, to harvest (perfective)

Для опроса нужно **собрать** и проанализировать много информации.
It's needed **to gather** and analyze lots of information for the survey.

1302 - Наступить [nastu'pit'] - *To come, to begin; to step on*

Почему лето не может **наступить** быстрее? Я так устала от холода!
Why can't summer **come** sooner? I'm so tired of the cold!

1303 - Покой [pa'koj] - *Calm, rest, peace*

После такого стрессового дня на работе мне нужен абсолютный **покой**.
After such a stressful day at work I need an absolute **calm**.

1304 - Тянуть [tja'nut'] - *To pull, to drag*

Когда клюёт, нужно **тянуть** удочку сильнее.
When it bites you should **pull** the rod harder.

1305 - Народный [na'rodnyj] - *People's; national; folk*

Верховный **народный** суд отказался рассматривать это дело.
The Supreme **People's** Court refused to hear the case.

1306 - Процент [pra'tsent] - *Percentage, percent*

В африканских странах большой **процент** населения остаётся неграмотным.
In African countries a great **percentage** of the population remains illiterate.

1307 - Постоянно [pasta'jannə] - *Constantly, always*

Ты **постоянно** теряешь свои ключи!
You're **constantly** losing your keys!

1308 - Бросать [bra'sat'] - *To give up; to throw*

Тебе пора **бросать** есть так много сладкого! Это вредно для здоровья!
It's time for you **to give up** eating so many sweet things! It's bad for health!

1309 - Мечтать [metch'tat'] - *To dream*

Я не могла даже **мечтать** о таком подарке! Огромное спасибо!
I couldn't even **dream** of such a present! Thanks a lot!

1310 - Захотеть [zaha'tet'] - *To want (to begin to want)*

Тебе нужно только **захотеть** этого, и у тебя всё получится.
You should only **want** it and you'll succeed.

1311 - Автобус [af'tobus] - *A bus*

Я опоздала на **автобус**, теперь мне придётся ждать ещё целый час.

I've missed the **bus** and now I'll have to wait for a whole hour.

1312 - Восток [vas'tok] - *East*

Восток страны был оккупирован врагом.

The **East** of the country was occupied by the enemy.

1313 - Оставлять [astav'ljat'] - *To leave; to abandon*

Я не хочу **оставлять** её одну в этот трудный период.

I don't want **to leave** her alone during this hard period.

1314 - Усмехнуться [usmeh'nutsa] - *To grin, to smile*

Его истории всегда заставляют меня **усмехнуться**.

His stories always make me **grin**.

1315 - Эхо ['ɛhə] - *An echo*

Мы слышали **эхо** наших голосов с другой стороны долины.

We heard the **echo** of our voices from the other side of the valley.

1316 - Примерно [pri'mernə] - *Approximately, about*

Этот магазин **примерно** в километре отсюда.

This shop is **approximately** a kilometer away from here.

1317 - Автомобиль [avtama'bil'] - *A car, an automobile*

Это гоночный **автомобиль** новой модели.

It's a new model race **car**.

1318 - Внешний ['vneshnyj] - *Outer, external*

Внутренний мир человека важнее, чем **внешний**.

The inner world of a person is more important than the **outer** one.

1319 - Технический [teh'nitcheskij] - *Technical*

Технический прогресс сильно изменил наш мир.
Technical progress has greatly changed our world.

1320 - Пропасть [pro'past'] - To get lost, to go missing; to disappear

Группа туристов могла **пропасть** в горах, но никто не уверен.
The group of tourists could **get lost** in the mountains but nobody is sure.

1321 - Выдержать ['vyderzhat'] - *To stand, to bear, to endure*

Их брак не смог **выдержать** проверку временем.
Their marriage was unable **to stand** the test of time.

1322 - Миг [mig] - An instant, a wink, a moment

Наша жизнь – это лишь **миг** в истории человечества.
Our life is just an **instant** in the history of mankind.

1323 - Отряд [at'rjad] - *A squad, a unit, a team*

Отряд полиции задержал грабителей прямо на месте преступления.
The police **squad** detained the robbers right at the crime scene.

1324 - Сверху ['sverhu] - On top; from above; above, over

Я хочу этот торт с клубникой **сверху**.
I want this cake with strawberries **on top**.

1325 - Настолько [nas'tol'kə] - *So, so much*

Ребёнок был **настолько** напуган, что не мог сказать ни слова.
The child was **so** scared that he couldn't say a word.

1326 - Встречать [vstre'tchat'] - *To meet; to greet, to welcome*

Всегда приятно **встречать** интересных людей.

It's always nice **to meet** interesting people.

1327 - Пускать [pus'kat'] - *To let in; to permit*

Они отказались меня **пускать**.

They refused **to let** me **in**.

1328 - Ясный ['jasnyj] - *Clear; bright*

Она дала **ясный** и детальный ответ.

She gave a **clear** and detailed answer.

1329 - Занятие [za'njatije] - *An occupation, a business; a lesson*

Ты бездельничаешь весь день! Найди себе какое-нибудь **занятие**!

You've been idling all day! Find yourself an **occupation**!

1330 - Реальный [re'al'nyj] - *Real*

Это невероятно! Неужели это **реальный** человек, а не выдумка?

It's unbelievable! Can it be a **real** man and not some fiction?

1331 - Задний ['zadnij] - *Back, rear*

Наш **задний** дворик уютный и тихий. Я люблю проводить там время.

Our **back** yard is cozy and quiet. I like to spend time there.

1332 - Европа [jev'ropa] - *Europe*

Европа окружена морями с трёх сторон.

Europe is surrounded by seas on three sides.

1333 - Случайно [slu'tchajnə] - *Accidentally, by accident*

Извини, я **случайно** разбил твою любимую чашку.
Sorry, I've **accidentally** broken your favorite cup.

1334 - Артист [ar'tist] - *An artist, a performer*

Народный **артист** – это почётное звание.
A people's **artist** is an honorary title.

1335 - Сложный ['slozhnyj] - *Complicated, difficult, complex*

Этот текст слишком **сложный** для студентов твоего уровня.
This text is too **complicated** for the students of your level.

1336 - Планета [pla'neta] - *A planet*

Юпитер – это самая большая **планета** Солнечной системы.
Jupiter is the biggest **planet** of the solar system.

1337 - Порог [pa'rog] - *A doorstep, a threshold*

Он отвратительный человек. Я не хочу даже пускать его на свой **порог**.
He's a disgusting person. I don't even want to let him get to my **doorstep**.

1338 - Явление [jav'lenije] - *A phenomenon*

Солнечное затмение – редкое и красивое **явление**.
A Solar eclipse is a rare and beautiful **phenomenon**.

1339 - Отпустить [atpus'tit'] - *To let go*

Чтобы идти дальше, тебе нужно **отпустить** своё прошлое.
To go on you should **let go** of your past.

1340 - Красота [krasa'ta] - *Beauty*

Красота этого пейзажа поразительна!
The **beauty** of this scenery is stunning!

1341 - Воскликнуть [vas'kliknut'] - *To exclaim, to cry*

Когда я увидела это платье, мне хотелось **воскликнуть**: "Вот то, что нужно!"
When I saw that dress I wanted **to exclaim**: 'That's what I need!'

1342 - Напротив [nap'rotiv] - *On the contrary*

Я не против твоей идеи, **напротив**, она мне очень нравится.
I'm not against your idea; **on the contrary,** I like it a lot.

1343 - Дрожать [dra'zhat'] - *To tremble, to shiver, to shake*

Я очень боюсь змей. Только один их вид заставляет меня **дрожать**.
I'm very much scared of snakes. The only sight of them makes me **tremble**.

1344 - Палатка [pa'latka] - *A tent*

Эта туристическая **палатка** водонепроницаемая и очень прочная.
This tourist **tent** is waterproof and very robust.

1345 - Выбрать ['vybrat'] - *To choose, to select (perfective)*

Я не смог **выбрать** правильный ответ на последний вопрос, но всё равно сдал тест.
I didn't manage **to choose** the correct answer to the last question, but still passed the test.

1346 - Пьяный ['pjanyj] - *Drunk; a drunk man*

Ты **пьяный** и не можешь садиться за руль.
You're **drunk** and can't drive.

1347 - Рада ['rada] - *Rada*

Парламент Украины называется **Рада**.
The parliament of Ukraine is called **Rada**.

1348 - Доска [das'ka] - **A board, a plate; a blackboard**

Эта разделочная **доска** сделана из натурального дерева.
This cutting **board** is made of natural wood.

1349 - Пистолет [pista'let] - *A pistol, a handgun*

Этот **пистолет** – главная улика расследования.
This **pistol** is the main piece of evidence of the investigation.

1350 - Пожать [pa'zhat'] - To shake; to reap (perfective)

Позвольте мне **пожать** Вашу мужественную руку!
Let me **shake** your courageous hand.

1351 - Актёр [ak'tjor] - *An actor*

Этот **актёр** так талантлив! Каждая его новая роль – это шедевр!
This **actor** is so talented! His every new role is a masterpiece!

1352 - Раздаться [raz'datsa] - To ring out (often unexpectedly)

Сейчас должен **раздаться** телефонный звонок. Я жду его весь день.
A phone call should **ring out** now. I've been waiting for it the whole day.

1353 - Зря [zrja] - *In vain, for nothing*

Мы **зря** пытались изменить его мнение. Он был упрям, как всегда.

We tried **in vain** to change his mind. He was stubborn, as usual.

1354 - Потолок [pata'lok] - *A ceiling*

Потолок в комнате слишком низкий, и поэтому она кажется маленькой.

The **ceiling** in the room is too low and that's why it seems small.

1355 - Постель [pas'tel'] - *A bed; bedding*

Сегодня я проспала и не успела **застелить** постель.

I overslept today and didn't have time to make my **bed**.

1356 - Навстречу [navst'retchu] - *Toward, towards*

Переезд в другой город стал для нас первым шагом **навстречу** большим переменам.

Moving to a different city became a first step **toward** big changes for us.

1357 - Ближайший [bli'zhajshij] - *Nearest; next*

Скажите пожалуйста, где находится **ближайший** банк?

Could you tell me please where the **nearest** bank is?

1358 - Сумка ['sumka] - *A bag, a handbag*

Эта **сумка** компактная и довольно вместительная.

This **bag** is compact and quite spacious.

1359 - Мгновение [mgna'venije] - An instant, a moment (synonymous to 'миг')

Лето прошло быстро, в одно **мгновение**.

The summer passed fast, in an **instant**.

1360 - Праздник ['praznik] - *A holiday*

Новый Год – это традиционный семейный **праздник**.
New Year is a traditional family **holiday**.

1361 - Густо ['gustə] - *Densely, thickly*

Индия – одна из самых **густо**населённых стран.
India is one of the most **densely** populated countries.

1362 - Мост [most] - *A bridge*

Мост через реку соединяет две части города.
The **bridge** across the river connects the two parts of the city.

1363 - Энергия [ɛ'nergija] - *Energy, power*

Завтрак для меня – это **энергия** дня.
Breakfast is the **energy** of the day for me.

1364 - Начальство [na'tchal'stvə] - *Boss, authority (collective)*

Здорово быть фрилансером – ты сам себе **начальство**.
It's great to be a freelancer – you're your own **boss**.

1365 - Сожаление [sozha'lenije] - *Regret, pity*

Я слышу **сожаление** в твоём голосе. Ты не рада, что приехала сюда?
I hear **regret** in your voice. Are you unhappy about coming here?

1366 - Полтора [palta'ra] - *One and a half*

Я освобожусь через **полтора** часа.
I'll be free in **an hour and a half**.

1367 - Объяснять [abjas'njat'] - *To explain, to clarify*

Тебе не нужно **объяснять** мне, каково это – не иметь работы. Я знаю это по своему опыту.

You don't need **to explain** it to me what it feels like to be out of work. I know it from experience.

1368 - Обращать [abrast'chat'] - *To pay, to turn*

Не стоит **обращать** внимание на то, что говорят другие.

It's not worth **paying** attention to what other people say.

1369 - Сунуть ['sunut'] - *To stick, to poke*

Мои родители используют любую возможность **сунуть** свой нос в мою личную жизнь.

My parents make use of any opportunity **to stick** their noses in my personal life.

1370 - Пятнадцать [pjat'nadtsat'] - *Fifteen*

Такси приедет через **пятнадцать** минут. Ты готова?
The taxi will arrive in **fifteen** minutes. Are you ready?

1371 - Разрешить [razre'shit'] - *To allow, to permit, to let*

Я не могу **разрешить** тебе играть с этим. Этот сувенир мне очень дорог.

I can't **allow** you to play with it. This souvenir is very dear to me.

1372 - Участок [u'tchastək] - *A stretch, a piece of land*

Этот **участок** дороги самый опасный.
This **stretch** of road is the most dangerous one.

1373 - Жертва ['zhertva] - *A victim; a sacrifice*

В этой ситуации я всего лишь **жертва** обстоятельств.
In this situation I'm just **a victim** of circumstances.

1374 - Меч [mjetch] - *A sword*

«**Меч** короля Артура» – это очень популярная легенда.
"King Arthur's **sword**" is a very popular legend.

1375 - Звонок [zva'nok] - *A call, a ring*

Я жду важный деловой **звонок**.
I'm expecting an important business **call**.

1376 - Кино [ki'no] - Cinema; a movie, a film

Сегодня вечером мы идём в **кино**. Ты с нами?
We're going to the **cinema** today. Are you with us?

1377 - Признаться [priz'natsa] - *To admit, to confess*

Я должен **признаться**, у тебя богатое воображение.
I must **admit** you've got a rich imagination.

1378 - Мороз [ma'roz] - Frost, freezing weather

Сильный **мороз** побил посевы.
The heavy **frost** damaged the crops.

1379 - Составлять [sastav'ljat'] - To constitute, to comprise; to construct, to compose

Все государственные органы должны **составлять** единую систему.
All the state organs must **constitute** a unified system.

1380 - Бедный ['bednyj] - Poor (both financially and defined by other circumstances)

Мой отец слишком **бедный**, чтобы позволить себе такую машину.
My father is too **poor** to afford such a car.

1381 - Летний ['ljetnij] - *Summer (adj)*

В августе я еду в **летний** лагерь.

I'm going to a **summer** camp in August.

1382 - Видать [vi'dat'] - *To see (colloquial)*

Мне отсюда не **видать**, едет его машина или нет.

I can't **see** from here if his car is coming or not.

1383 - Адрес ['adres] - *An address*

Пришли мне свой новый **адрес** в сообщении, пожалуйста.

Please, send me your new **address** in a message.

1384 - Закрытый [zak'rytyj] - *Closed; secret*

Для эксперимента вам понадобится **закрытый** сосуд.

You'll need a **closed** vessel for the experiment.

1385 Горло ['gorlə] - *A throat*

У меня ужасно болит **горло**, и я едва могу разговаривать.

I have a terrible sore **throat** and I can barely talk.

1386 - Костёр [kas'tjor] - A fire, a bonfire, a wood fire

Мы установили палатки, развели **костёр** и начали готовить.

We put up our tents, made **a fire** and started cooking.

1387 - Жалко ['zhalkə] - It is a pity, unfortunately

Жалко, что ты не сможешь прийти ко мне на день рождения.

It is a pity you won't be able to come to my birthday party.

1388 - Кот [kot] - *A cat (male)*

Наш **кот** не ест ничего, кроме рыбы.

Our **cat** doesn't eat anything except fish.

1389 - Бык [byk] - *A bull, an ox*

Бык – это упрямое животное, которое может быть довольно опасным.

A **bull** is a stubborn animal that can be quite dangerous.

1390 - Трудный ['trudnyj] - *Hard, difficult*

Ей пришлось сделать **трудный** выбор между любовью и карьерой.

She had to make a **difficult** choice between love and her career.

1391 - Текст [tekst] - *A text*

Этот простой **текст** подойдёт начинающим.

This simple **text** will be suitable for beginners.

1392 - Тепло [tep'lo] - Warmth; it is warm (impersonal about weather)

Детям больше всего нужно внимание и **тепло** родителей.

Children need the attention and **warmth** of their parents most of all.

1393 - Занимать [zani'mat'] - To occupy, to take up; to borrow

Я думаю, этот шкаф будет **занимать** слишком много места в нашей спальне.

I think this wardrobe will **occupy** too much space in our bedroom.

1394 - Песок [pe'sok] - *Sand*

Тёплый **песок**, яркое солнце – день на пляже был идеальным.

The warm **sand**, the bright sun – the day at the beach was perfect.

1395 - Больно ['bol'nə] - Painful, painfully; bad, badly

Мне **больно** это говорить, но я думаю, нам стоит расстаться.

It's **painful** for me to say it but I think we should break up.

1396 - Сомнение [sam'nenije] - *A doubt*

Если у тебя есть хоть одно **сомнение**, то не спеши принимать решение.

If you have even a single **doubt**, don't be in a hurry to make the decision.

1397 - Территория [teri'torija] - *A territory, an area*

Территория страны разделена на несколько провинций.

The **territory** of the country is divided into several provinces.

1398 - Тайна ['tajna] - *A secret; a mystery*

Это будет наша с тобой **тайна**. Никто не должен узнать об этом.

It's going to be our **secret**. Nobody must learn about it.

1399 - Волк [volk] - *A wolf*

Ночью **волк** напал на стадо и убил несколько овец.

A **wolf** attacked the herd at night and killed a few sheep.

1400 - Терять [te'rjat'] - *To lose*

Я уезжаю из страны. Мне всё равно нечего **терять**.

I'm leaving the country. I have nothing **to lose** anyway.

1401 - Приятель [pri'jatel'] - *A fellow, a mate*

Он мой хороший **приятель**, но я не могу назвать его своим другом.

He's a good **fellow** of mine but I can't call him my friend.

1402 - Рукав [ru'kav] - *A sleeve*

Мне кажется, правый **рукав** этой рубашки короче, чем левый.

It seems to me that the right **sleeve** of this shirt is shorter than the left one.

1403 - Дедушка ['dedushka] - *A grandfather, a granddad*

Когда мы были детьми, **дедушка** много играл с нами.
When we were kids, our **grandfather** played with us a lot.

1404 - Вскочить [vska'tchit'] - **To leap (up, onto, to), to jump (up, onto), to get up quickly**

Не успел я **вскочить** на ноги, как соперник ударил меня снова.
Hardly had I managed **to leap** to my feet when my opponent hit me again.

1405 - Прочитать [prachi'tat'] - **To read, to read through (perfective)**

У меня не было времени **прочитать** книгу до конца. Можно мне оставить её ещё на день?
I had no time **to read** the book till the end. May I keep it for another day?

1406 - Честно ['tchesnə] - **Honestly, frankly; fair, fairly**

Честно говоря, я не в настроении идти на дискотеку.
Honestly speaking, I'm not in the mood to go to the disco.

1407 - Масло ['maslə] - *Butter; oil*

Закончилось **масло**. Добавь его в список покупок.
We've run out of **butter**. Add it to the shopping list.

1408 - Постоянный [pasta'jannyj] - *Constant, permanent*

Постоянный контроль родителей действует мне на нервы.
My parents' **constant** control is getting on my nerves.

1409 - Всякая ['fsjakaja] - All sorts of, all kinds of; any (feminine of `всякий)

В этом ящике у меня хранится **всякая** всячина типа открыток, марок и старых билетов.

In this drawer I keep **all sorts of** stuff like postcards, stamps and old tickets.

1410 - Существование [sustchestva'vanije] - *Existence, being*

Я не верю в **существование** инопланетян. А ты?

I don't believe in the **existence** of aliens. And you?

1411 - Лезть [lest'] - To climb (up, onto); to intrude

Пожарному пришлось **лезть** на дерево, чтобы снять кошку.

The fireman had **to climb** up the tree to put the cat down.

1412 - Младший ['mladshij] - *Younger; junior*

Мой **младший** брат ходит в детский сад.

My **younger** brother goes to the kindergarten.

1413 - Отправить [at'pravit'] - *To send (perfective)*

Скажите пожалуйста, какие бумаги мне нужно заполнить, чтобы **отправить** посылку за границу?

Tell me please, what papers should I fill in **to send** a parcel abroad?

1414 - Построить [past'roit'] - To build, to construct (perfective)

Мне интересно, как древние египтяне смогли **построить** пирамиды без современного оборудования.

I wonder how ancient Egyptians managed to **build** the pyramids without modern equipment.

1415 - Нервный ['nervnyj] - *Nervous*

Почему ты такой **нервный** сегодня? Что-нибудь случилось?
Why are you so **nervous** today? Has anything happened?

1416 - Пустить ['pustit'] - To let, to allow, to permit; to let in (perfective)

Я не могу **пустить** тебя на прогулку одну так поздно.
I can't **let** you go for a walk alone so late.

1417 - Рождение [razh'denije] - *Birth*

Рождение нового человека – это удивительное событие в жизни каждой семьи.
The **birth** of a new person is an amazing event in the life of every family.

1418 - Заглянуть [zaglja'nut'] - To peep in, to glance at; to drop by, to call on (colloquial)

У моей бабушки был большой старый сундук. Мне всегда хотелось **заглянуть** в него.
My grandmother had a large old chest. I always wanted **to peep** into it.

1419 - Проговорить [pragava'rit'] - *To talk (for a long time)*

Мы могли **проговорить** всю ночь и не заметить этого.
We could **talk** the whole night and not notice it.

1420 - Воспоминание [vaspəmi'nanije] - *A memory, a recollection*

День нашей встречи – это моё любимое **воспоминание**.
The day we met is my favorite **memory**.

1421 - Проверить [pra'verit'] - *To check (perfective)*

Не забудь **проверить**, выключил ли ты свет перед уходом.
Don't forget **to check** if you've switched off the lights before leaving.

1422 - Болеть [ba'let'] - **To be ill, to be sick; to cheer for**

Я ненавижу **болеть** летом, когда все плавают и загорают.
I hate **being ill** in summer when everyone's swimming and sunbathing.

1423 - Тон [ton] - **A tone (of voice, music, color)**

Мне не нравится твой **тон**. Не разговаривай со мной так грубо.
I don't like your **tone**. Don't talk to me so rudely.

1424 - Понятие [pan''jatije] - *A concept, an idea*

Попробуйте объяснить это научное **понятие** сами.
Try to explain this scientific **concept** yourselves.

1425 - Низкий ['niskij] - *Low; short (of a person)*

В этом городе очень **низкий** уровень преступности.
This city has a very **low** crime rate.

1426 - Далее ['daleje] - **Then; further, furthermore; farther**

Прочтите текст и **далее** ответьте на вопросы.
Read the text and **then** answer the questions.

1427 - Вечный ['vechnyj] - *Eternal, everlasting*

Я молюсь за **вечный** мир на земле.
I pray for **eternal** peace on Earth.

1428 - Песня ['pjesnja] - *A song*

О, это моя любимая **песня**! Сделай громче!

Oh, that's my favorite **song**! Turn it up!

1429 - Морской [mar'skoj] - *Sea, seaside (adj)*

Дул свежий **морской** бриз, и мы гуляли по набережной.

A fresh **sea** breeze was blowing and we were walking along the quay.

1430 - Крыло [kry'lo] - *A wing*

Крыло птицы зажило, и мы выпустили её на волю.

The bird's **wing** healed and we let it out into the wild.

1431 - Поднимать [padni'mat'] - *To lift, to raise, to elevate*

Тебе нельзя **поднимать** такие тяжёлые вещи. Дай я помогу тебе.

You can't **lift** such heavy things. Let me help you.

1432 - Розовый ['rozavyj] - *Pink*

Розовый – цвет моды и гламура, но мне он не нравится.

Pink is the color of fashion and glamour but I don't like it.

1433 - Нарушение [naru'shenije] - *Violation, breach*

Это **нарушение** прав человека, и с этим нельзя мириться.

It's the **violation** of human rights and it can't be put up with.

1434 - Осень ['osen'] - *Autumn*

Осень – удивительно красивая, красочная пора года.

Autumn is an amazingly beautiful and colorful season of the year.

1435 - Положенный [pa'lozhennyj] - *Due*

Постарайтесь подготовить все бумаги в **положенный** срок.
Try to prepare all the papers in **due** time.

1436 - Туман [tu'man] - *Fog*

Туман был таким густым, что мы ничего не видели.
The **fog** was so dense that we couldn't see anything.

1437 - Ленинград [lenin'grad] - *Leningrad*

В советское время Санкт-Петербург назывался **Ленинград**.
In Soviet times, St. Petersburg was called **Leningrad**.

1438 - Платье ['plat'je] - *A dress*

Я купила новое **платье**, и теперь мне нужна подходящая сумочка.
I've bought a new **dress** and now I need a handbag to match.

1439 - Представление [pretstav'lenije] - *A performance*

Это было лучшее цирковое **представление**, которое я только видел!
That was the best circus **performance** I've ever seen!

1440 - Изменение [izme'nenije] - A change, a modification, an alteration

В правилах есть небольшое **изменение**. Будьте внимательны.
There's a slight **change** in the rules. Be attentive.

1441 - Вариант [vari'ant] - *An option, a variant*

Посмотрите на этот **диван**. Это более доступный вариант.
Have a look at this **sofa**. It' a more affordable option.

1442 - Шофёр [sha'fjor] - *A chauffeur, a driver*

Мой сосед такой богатый, что у него есть *личный* **шофёр**.
My neighbor is so rich that he has a personal **chauffeur**.

1443 - Опасный [a'pasnyj] - *Dangerous*

Снизь скорость – впереди **опасный** поворот.
Slow down – there's a **dangerous** turn ahead.

1444 - Означать [azna'tchat'] - *To mean*

Я не могу понять, что бы могла **означать** её фраза. Она точно что-то скрывает от нас.
I can't understand what her phrase could **mean**. She's surely hiding something from us.

1445 - Вход [fhot] - *An entrance, an entry*

Убери эти коробки отсюда. Они загораживают **вход** в дом.
Take these boxes away from here. They're blocking the **entrance** to the house.

1446 - Практически [prak'titcheski] - *Almost; virtually, practically*

Практически все наши сбережения были потрачены на восстановление дома после пожара.
Almost all our savings were spent on the reconstruction of the house after the fire.

1447 - Нынешний ['nyneshnij] - *Present, today's*

Наш **нынешний** начальник гораздо более требовательный, чем предыдущий.
Our **present** boss is much more demanding than the former one.

1448 - Глупо ['glupə] - *Silly, foolishly*

Было **глупо** с твоей стороны обижаться на его шутку.
That was **silly** of you to be offended by his joke.

1449 - Национальный [natsia'nal'nyj] - *National*

На церемонии открытия спортсмены спели свой
национальный гимн.
At the opening ceremony, the sportsmen sang their **national**
anthem.

1450 - Чиновник [tchi'novnik] - *An official, a functionary*

Этот **чиновник** обвиняется во взяточничестве.
This **official** is accused of bribery.

1451 - Поверхность [pa'verhnəst'] - *A surface*

Поверхность этого кожаного чемодана гладкая и блестящая.
The **surface** of this leather suitcase is smooth and glossy.

1452 - Приятный [pri'jatnyj] - *Pleasant, pleasing, agreeable*

Приятный звук музыки помог мне успокоиться и
расслабиться.
The **pleasant** sound of the music helped me to calm down and
relax.

1453 - Каменный ['kamennyj] - *Stone (adj); stony*

Этот старинный **каменный** мост был построен в тринадцатом
веке.
This ancient **stone** bridge was built in the thirteenth century.

1454 - Говориться [gava'ritsa] - To say (impersonal), to be said, to be about

В инструкции должно **говориться**, как правильно чистить прибор.

The instructions must **say** how to clean the device correctly.

1455 - Прочий ['prochij] - *Other*

В резюме следует указать ваше образование, предыдущее место работы и **прочий** опыт.

You should state your education, previous employment and **other** experience in the CV.

1456 - Испытывать [is'pytyvat'] - *To experience, to feel; to test*

Должно быть, сложно **испытывать** столько разных эмоций одновременно.

It must be hard **to experience** so many different emotions at a time.

1457 - Рано ['ranə] - *Early*

Я пришел слишком **рано**, и мне пришлось ждать, пока магазин откроется.

I came too **early** and had to wait before the shop opens.

1458 - Жениться [zhe'nitsa] - To get married (of a couple when they marry each other) or to marry somebody (of a man when he takes a wife)

Мы встречаемся ещё только несколько месяцев и не хотим **жениться** так скоро.

We've been dating for a few months only and don't want **to get married** so soon.

1459 - Аппарат [apa'rat] - An apparatus, a device; an apparat (political)

Учёный изобрёл сложный **аппарат** и получил за него международную премию.

The scientist invented a complex **apparatus** and received an international award for it.

1460 - Церковь ['tserkof'] - A church (both an institution and a building)

Церковь всегда играла важную роль в истории России.

The **church** has always played an important role in the history of Russia.

1461 - Ручка ['rutchka] - *A handle, a knob; a pen*

Эта деревянная **ручка** нелепо смотрится на металлической двери.

This wooden **handle** looks awkward on the metal door.

1462 - Оглянуться [aglja'nutsa] - To look back, to turn back (both literally and figuratively)

Иногда приятно **оглянуться** и вспомнить прошлое.

Sometimes it's nice **to look back** and remember the past.

1463 - Пригласить [prigla'sit'] - *To invite (perfective)*

Сколько гостей вы планируете **пригласить** на свадьбу?

How many guests are you planning **to invite** to the wedding?

1464 - Хозяйка [ha'z'ajka] - A hostess; an owner (female); a wife (colloquial)

Вечеринка была отличной, а **хозяйка** выглядела очаровательно.

The party was great and the **hostess** looked charming.

1465 - Строго ['strogə] - *Strictly*

Не смотри на меня так **строго**. Это всего лишь разбитая чашка.

Don't look at me so **strictly**. It's just a broken cup.

1466 - Принадлежать [prinadle'zhat'] - *To belong*

Этот дневник не может **принадлежать** твоему брату. На нём другое имя.

This diary can't **belong** to your brother. It has a different name on it.

1467 - Внезапный [vne'zapnyj] - *Sudden, unexpected*

Внезапный ливень застал нас в поле, и нам негде было спрятаться.

A **sudden** rain shower caught us in the field and we had nowhere to hide.

1468 - Единый [je'dinyj] - *Unified, single; united*

Невозможно найти **единый** подход ко всем ученикам. Каждый из них – личность.

It's impossible to find a **unified** approach to all pupils. Each of them is a personality.

1469 - Дворец [dva'rets] - *A palace*

Этот средневековый **дворец** – часть культурного наследия страны.

This medieval **palace** is part of the cultural heritage of the country.

1470 - Водитель [va'ditel'] - *A driver*

Водитель потерял управление и врезался в фонарный столб.

The **driver** lost control of the car and crashed into a lamp post.

1471 - Строить ['stroit'] - *To build, to construct*

Здесь собираются **строить** новый торговый центр.
A new mall is going **to be built** here.

1472 - Множество ['mnozhestvə] - *A multitude, a variety*

В мире **множество** животных и растений, о которых мы ничего не знаем.
There's a **multitude** of animals and plants in the world we don't know anything about.

1473 - Перейти [perej'ti] - *To cross, to get over; to pass on to*

Я не могу найти, где **перейти** дорогу. Где здесь пешеходный переход?
I can't find where **to cross** the road. Where's a zebra crossing here?

1474 - Столик ['stolik] - *A table (diminutive, a little table, very often in the context of booking a table in a restaurant)*

На день святого Валентина мы заказали **столик** в ресторане.
On Valentine's Day we booked **a table** in a restaurant.

1475 - Урок [u'rok] - *A lesson*

Стандартный **урок** в русской школе длится 45 минут.
A standard **lesson** in a Russian school lasts 45 minutes.

1476 - Древний ['drevnij] - *Ancient*

Ежегодно этот **древний** греческий храм посещают тысячи туристов.
Thousands of tourists visit this **ancient** Greek temple annually.

1477 - Опасность [a'pasnəst'] - *Danger, risk*

Опасность курения очевидна, но, похоже, многих курильщиков это не волнует.

The **danger** of smoking is evident but it looks like many smokers don't care about it.

1478 - Повезти [paves'ti] - To be lucky, to have luck (impersonal)

Как ей могло так **повезти**? Она опять выиграла в лотерею!

How could she **be** so **lucky**? She's won the lottery again!

1479 - Французский [fran'tsuskij] - *The French language; French*

Французский считается языком любви.

The **French language** is considered to be the language of love.

1480 - Поглядеть [paglja'det'] - To have a look at, to glance at (quickly, not for long)

Можно **поглядеть** на вашего малыша?

May I **have a look at** your baby?

1481 - Горе ['gore] - Misfortune, grief, trouble

Её муж умер от сердечного приступа. Какое **горе**!

Her husband died of a heart attack. What a **misfortune**!

1482 - Честный ['tchesnyj] - *Honest; fair*

Я ценю твой **честный** ответ.

I appreciate your **honest** answer.

1483 - Способность [spa'sobnast'] - *An ability, a capability*

У тебя есть удивительная **способность** понимать меня в любой ситуации.

You have an amazing **ability** to understand me in any situation.

1484 - Повернуть [paver''nut'] - To turn (both transitive and intransitive)

На перекрёстке вам нужно будет **повернуть** направо, и вы сразу же увидите это здание.

You'll need **to turn** right at the crossroads and you'll see the building at once.

1485 - Остальное [astal''noje] - *The rest*

Я ставлю свою семью на первое место, **остальное** для меня не важно.

I place my family at the first place, **the rest** doesn't matter to me.

1486 - Добраться [dab'ratsa] - *To get to, to reach*

Мы не успеем **добраться** до аэропорта вовремя, если немного не поторопимся .

We won't manage **to get to** the airport in time if we don't hurry a bit.

1487 - Серьёзно [ser''joznə] - *Seriously, earnestly*

Не воспринимай его слова так **серьёзно**. Он просто шутит.

Don't take his words so **seriously**. He's just joking.

1488 - Признать [priz'nat'] - To admit; to acknowledge (perfective)

Мне было нелегко **признать** свою вину, но я рад, что сделал это.

It was uneasy for me **to admit** my guilt but I'm happy I did it.

1489 - Поступить [pastu'pit'] - To act, to behave; to enter, to join (perfective)

Я не знаю, как **поступить** в этой ситуации. Ты можешь дать мне совет?

I don't know how **to act** in this situation. Can you give me advice?

1490 - Работник [ra'botnik] - A worker, an employee (blue-collar)

Вы отличный **работник**, и, я думаю, вы заслуживаете повышение.

You're an excellent **worker** and I think you deserve a promotion.

1491 - Долг [dolg] - *A duty; a debt*

Помочь родителям в старости – мой **долг**.

Helping my parents in their old age is my **duty**.

1492 - Специалист [spetsia'list] - *A specialist, an expert*

Нам нужен квалифицированный **специалист** с большим опытом.

We need a **qualified** specialist with lots of experience.

1493 - Торопиться [tara'pitsa] - *To hurry, to be in a hurry*

Не нужно **торопиться** – у нас много времени.

There's no need **to hurry** – we've got plenty of time.

1494 - Итак [i'tak] - *So, then*

Итак, где мы остановились?

So, where did we stop?

1495 - Центральный [tsen'tral'nyj] - *Central*

Во время праздника **центральный** парк был переполнен людьми.

During the fest the **central** park was crowded with people.

1496 - Телевизор [tele'vizər] - *A TV set*

Давай купим современный **телевизор** с плоским экраном.

Let's buy a modern flat screen **TV set**.

1497 - Зло [zlo] - *Evil, bad*

В сказках добро всегда побеждает **зло**.
In fairy tales good always triumphs over **evil**.

1498 - Вкус [fkus] - *A taste*

Я никогда не забуду **вкус** этих пирожных! Как ты их готовишь?
I'll never forget the **taste** of these cakes! How do you cook them?

1499 - Муха ['muha] - *A fly (an insect)*

Что за надоедливая **муха**! Как нам её прихлопнуть?
What a bothersome **fly**! How can we swat it?

1500 - Поиск ['poisk] - *A search*

Простой **поиск** в Интернете докажет, что ты ошибаешься.
A simple **search** on the Internet will prove that you're wrong.

1501 - Старшина [starshi'na] - *A sergeant major (a military rank)*

Старшина поприветствовал новобранцев.
The **sergeant major** greeted the recruits.

1502 - Озеро ['ozerə] - *A lake*

Горное **озеро** было чистым и прозрачным.
The mountain **lake** was pure and transparent.

1503 - Чемодан [tchema'dan] - *A suitcase*

Ты упаковала свой **чемодан**? Не забудь про тёплые вещи!
Have you packed your **suitcase**? Don't forget about the warm clothes!

1504 - Вынуть ['vynut'] - To take out, to pull out (colloquial)

Что за странный запах? Ты забыл **вынуть** пирог из духовки?
What kind of a strange smell is it? Have you forgotten **to take** the pie **out** of the oven?

1505 - Сзади ['zzadi] - Behind, from behind, in the back

Пассажиры **сзади** меня громко разговаривали всю дорогу!
The passengers **behind** me were talking loudly the whole way!

1506 - Стоить ['stoit'] - *To cost; to be worth*

Эти туфли не могут столько **стоить**! Я не собираюсь их покупать!
These shoes can't **cost** so much! I'm not going to buy them!

1507 - Предел [pre'del] - A limit, a boundary, a margin

У моего терпения есть **предел**. Я устала работать сверхурочно.
There's **a limit** to my patience. I'm tired of working overtime.

1508 - Музей [mu'zej] - *A museum*

На выходных мы посетили морской **музей**.
We visited a maritime **museum** at the weekend.

1509 - Пятно [pjat'no] - *A stain, a spot*

Я не могу вывести это жирное **пятно** со своей любимой блузки.
I can't get this grease **stain** out of my favorite blouse.

1510 - Зона ['zona] - A zone; a prison (slang)

Это радиоактивная **зона**. Здесь никто не живёт уже много лет.
It's a radiation **zone**. Nobody has been living here for many years.

1511 - Ученик [utche'nik] - *A pupil, a student*

Работать с этим мальчиком одно удовольствие! Он очень способный **ученик**.

Working with this boy is a sheer pleasure! He's a very gifted **pupil**.

1512 - Навсегда [navseg'da] - *Forever*

Я собирался пожить в Лондоне пару лет, а остался здесь **навсегда**.

I was going to live in London for a couple of years but stayed here **forever**.

1513 - Толк [tolk] - *A use, a sense*

Какой **толк** от твоих извинений? Они ничего не изменят.

What's the **use** of your apologies? They won't change anything.

1514 - Полагать [pala'gat'] - *To suppose, to believe, to recon*

У меня есть причина **полагать**, что подозреваемый не виноват.

I've got a reason **to suppose** that the suspect is not guilty.

1515 - Родственник ['rotstvenik] - *A relative*

Он мой дальний **родственник**, и я практически ничего не знаю о нём.

He's my distant **relative** and I know almost nothing about him.

1516 - Источник [is'tochnik] - *A source; a spring*

Этот веб сайт – ненадёжный **источник** информации.

This website is an unreliable **source** of information.

1517 - Угодно [u'godnə] - Most often used in a word combination 'какой угодно' - [ka'koj u'godnə] - Any, whichever, whatsoever

Давай, задай мне **какой угодно** вопрос! Я отвечу на всё!
Come on, ask me **any** question! I'll answer all of them!

1518 - Послушать [pas'lushat'] - To listen (to listen for some time)

Я хочу немного отдохнуть, **послушать** музыку и расслабиться.
I want to have some rest, **to listen** to some music and relax.

1519 - Колесо [kale'so] - *A wheel*

Я не знаю, кто изобрёл **колесо**, но этот человек был гений.
I don't know who invented the **wheel** but that man was a genius.

1520 - Грязь [gr'as'] - *Mud, filth, dirt*

На твоих ботинках **грязь**. Не забудь почистить их.
There's **mud** on your shoes. Don't forget to clean them.

1521 - Отметить [at'metit'] - To celebrate; to point out; to mark

Я хочу **отметить** Новый год в семейном кругу.
I want **to celebrate** the New Year within the family circle.

1522 - Стен [sten] - A wall (in genitive plural of 'стена')

Из-за сырости обои отклеились от **стен**.
The wallpaper peeled off the **walls** because of dampness.

1523 - Добро [dab'ro] - *The good*

Он всегда стремился делать людям **добро**, несмотря ни на что.
He's always strived to do people **good**, no matter what.

1524 - Капля ['kaplja] - *A drop; a bit*

Говорят, что **капля** никотина может убить лошадь.
They say **a drop** of nicotine can kill a horse.

1525 - Экран [ɛk'ran] - *A screen*

Мне нужен телевизор побольше. У этого **экран** маленький.
I need a bigger TV set. This one has a small **screen**.

1526 - Руководитель [rukava'ditel'] - *A leader, a manager*

Настоящий *лидер* работает вместе со своей командой.
A real **leader** works together with his team.

1527 - Инспектор [ins'pektər] - *An inspector, a controller*

Инспектор остановил подозрительный автомобиль, который ехал слишком быстро.
The **inspector** stopped a suspicious car that was going too fast.

1528 - Удивление [udiv'lenije] - *Amazement, surprise*

Она не могла скрыть своё **удивление**, когда увидела, что мы убрали всю квартиру.
She couldn't hide her **amazement** when she saw that we'd cleaned the whole apartment.

1529 - Утверждать [utver'zhdat'] - *To claim, to argue*

Как ты можешь **утверждать**, что она виновата, если ты даже не знаешь, что случилось?
How can you **claim** that she's guilty if you don't even know what had happened?

1530 - Молоко [mala'ko] - *Milk*

Горячее **молоко** с мёдом поможет облегчить твой кашель.
Some hot **milk** with honey will help to relieve your cough.

1531 - Очевидно [atche'vidnə] - *Obviously, it is obvious*

Вы, **очевидно**, не совсем понимаете, что мы от вас хотим.
You **obviously** don't quite understand what we want from you.

1532 - Отличаться [atli'tchatsa] - *To differ*

Эти элементы не должны **отличаться** друг от друга по цвету и размеру.
These elements shouldn't **differ** from each other in color and size.

1533 - Предложение [predla'zhenije] - *An offer; a sentence*

Это очень интересное деловое **предложение**, но мне придётся отказаться.
It's a very interesting business **offer** but I'll have to decline.

1534 - Нету ['netu] - No, there is no, there are no (colloquial)

У меня совсем **нету** времени на пустые разговоры.
I have absolutely **no** time for empty talk.

1535 - Среда [sre'da] - Environment, surroundings; Wednesday

Этим растениям нужна особая **среда**.
These plants need a special **environment**.

1536 - Выскочить ['vyskatchit'] - *To jump out, to pop out*

Будь осторожен! Здесь на дорогу могут **выскочить** дикие животные.
Be careful! Wild animals can **jump out** onto the road here.

1537 - Одетый [a'detyj] - *Dressed*

На вечеринке был парень, **одетый** как пришелец.
At the party there was a guy **dressed** like an alien.

1538 - Площадка [pla'sthadka] - *A platform; a playground*

На верху здания есть смотровая **площадка**.
There's a viewing **platform** on the top of the building.

1539 - Приезжать [priez'zhat'] - To come, to arrive (by horse or vehicle)

Я люблю **приезжать** в родительский дом во время каникул.
I like **to come** to my parents' house during the holidays.

1540 - Катить [ka'tit'] - To roll, to push (an object with wheels)

В этом чемодане есть колёсики. Ты можешь **катить** его.
This suitcase has wheels. You can **roll** it.

1541 - Совесть ['sovest'] - *Conscience*

Если у тебя есть сомнения, слушай свою **совесть**.
If you have doubts, listen to your **conscience**.

1542 - Кофе ['kofe] - *Coffee*

Я не люблю **кофе** с сахаром. Он только портит вкус.
I don't like **coffee** with sugar. It only spoils the taste.

1543 - Штаны [shta'ny'] - Pants, trousers (more for casual style)

Эти **штаны** продаются со скидкой. Хочешь примерить их?
These **pants** are on discount. Want to try them on?

1544 - Охота [a'hota] - *Hunting*

Я считаю, что **охота** – это жестокое и бессмысленное развлечение.
I consider **hunting** to be cruel and senseless entertainment.

1545 - Бровь [brov'] - *An eyebrow*

Оса ужалила меня прямо в левую **бровь**.
A wasp stung me right on the left **eyebrow**.

1546 - Расти [ras'ti] - *To grow; to increase*

Эти деревья могут **расти** только в тропическом климате.
These trees can only **grow** in a tropical climate.

1547 - Список ['spisək] - *A list*

Проверь **список** гостей. Может, ты захочешь добавить кого-нибудь.
Check the guest **list**. Maybe you'll want to add someone.

1548 - Ниже ['nizhə] - *Below; lower*

Ниже вы найдёте все прикреплённые документы.
Below you'll find all the attached documents.

1549 - Вернуть [ver'nut'] - *To return, to give back*

Я постараюсь **вернуть** твою книгу как можно скорее.
I'll try **to return** your book as soon as possible.

1550 - Зависеть [za'viset'] - *To depend on*

Когда я была студенткой, я не хотела **зависеть** от родителей и нашла себе работу.
When I was a student, I didn't want **to depend** on my parents and found myself a job.

1551 - Ствол [stvol] - A trunk (of a tree); a gun (slang)

Ствол этого дерева просто огромный! Я не могу обхватить его руками.

The **trunk** of this tree is just huge! I can't put my arms around it.

1552 - Основание [asna'vanije] - *A ground, a reason; a basis*

У тебя есть хоть какое-нибудь **основание** не доверять мне?

Do you have at least any **ground** not to trust me?

1553 - Северный ['severnyj] - *Northern*

Северный район города сильно пострадал от вчерашнего града.

The **northern** district of the city suffered from yesterday's hail a lot.

1554 - Познакомиться [pazna'komitsa] - *To meet, to get acquainted*

Приятно **познакомиться** с вами! Я много слышал о вас от своей сестры.

Nice **to meet** you! I've heard a lot about you from my sister.

1555 - Поведение [pave'denije] - *Behavior*

Такое **поведение** просто неприемлемо! Нельзя вот так выходить из себя.

Such **behavior** is just unacceptable! One can't lose their temper like that.

1556 - Жалить ['zhalit'] - To sting (of insects); to bite (of snakes)

Пчела не будет **жалить**, если ты не будешь её трогать.

A bee won't **sting** you if you don't touch it.

1557 - Найтись [naj'tis'] - To be found, to be discovered (in passive)

Смотри, вот твоя серёжка! Она должна была **найтись** рано или поздно.

Look, here's your earring! It had **to be found** sooner or later.

1558 - Делаться ['delatsa] - *To be done, to be made*

Такая работа не должна **делаться** в спешке.

Such work mustn't **be done** in haste.

1559 - Догадаться [daga'datsa] - *To guess*

Он не должен **догадаться**, что мы готовим ему сюрприз.

He mustn't **guess** that we're planning a surprise for him.

1560 - Дальнейший [dal''nejshij] - *Further*

Дальнейший прогресс твоего выздоровления зависит только от тебя.

Further progress of your recovery depends only on you.

1561 - Прожить [pra'zhit'] - To live (for some time or to live a life)

Я хочу **прожить** долгую жизнь, поэтому забочусь о своём здоровье.

I want **to live** a long life which is why I care about my health.

1562 - Усилие [u'silije] - *An effort*

Ещё одно **усилие** – и мы сдвинем этот камень.

One more **effort,** and we'll move this stone.

1563 - Гулять [gu'ljat'] - To walk, to go for a walk, to stroll

Я люблю **гулять** по ночному городу.

I like **to walk** around the city at night.

1564 - Клетка ['kletka] - *A cage; a cell (biology)*

Мне нужна более просторная **клетка** для моего попугая.
I need a more spacious **cage** for my parrot.

1565 - Разобраться [razab'ratsa] - *To sort out; to understand*

Я не смогу **разобраться** с этой проблемой в одиночку. Мне нужна помощь.
I won't be able **to sort** this problem **out** alone. I need help.

1566 - Обращать [abrast'chat'] - To pay (most often about attention)

Постарайся не **обращать** внимания на его поведение. Он делает это нарочно.
Try not **to pay** attention to his behavior. He does it on purpose.

1567 - Верхний ['verhnij] - *Upper*

Верхний слой воды в озере тёплый, но глубже вода ледяная.
The **upper** layer of the water in the lake is warm but deeper down the water is icy cold.

1568 - Обстановка [absta'novka] - An atmosphere, a setting; decor, furniture

После ссоры **обстановка** в комнате была напряжённой.
After the quarrel the **atmosphere** in the room was tense.

1569 - Температура [tempera'tura] - T*emperature*

Температура кипящей воды – 100 градусов по Цельсию.
The **temperature** of boiling water is 100 degrees Celcius.

1570 - Вывод ['vyvət] - *A conclusion; withdrawal*

Не спеши делать **вывод**. Ты ещё не знаешь всех обстоятельств.
Don't hurry to make a **conclusion**. You don't know all the circumstances yet.

1571 - Абсолютно [absa'ljutnə] - *Absolutely, completely*

Я **абсолютно** уверен, что они помирятся.
I'm **absolutely** sure that they'll make up.

1572 - Предприятие [pretpri'jatije] - *An enterprise, a business*

Это семейное **предприятие**. Оно было открыто моим дедом семьдесят лет назад.
It's a family **enterprise**. It was opened by my grandfather seventy years ago.

1573 - Принятый ['prinjatyj] - *Adopted, accepted*

Мне кажется, что **принятый** вчера закон поможет развитию малого бизнеса.
It seems to me that the law **adopted** yesterday will help the development of the small business.

1574 - Отдавать [atda'vat'] - *To give back, to give, to return*

Девочка не хотела **отдавать** игрушку, которую взяла у друга в песочнице.
The girl didn't want **to give back** the toy she borrowed from a friend in the sandbox.

1575 - Сходить [sha'dit'] - *To go (perfective) (means to go and do something)*

Ты можешь **сходить** на кухню и принести печенье?
Can you **go to** the kitchen and bring the cookies?

1576 - Подарок [pa'darək] - *A gift, a present*

Сложно найти **подарок** для человека, у которого всё есть!
It's hard to find **a gift** for a person who has everything!

1577 - Звучать [zvu'tchat'] - *To sound*

Твои слова будут **звучать** убедительнее, если ты перестанешь кричать.

Your words will **sound** more persuasive if you stop yelling.

1578 - Отделение [atde'lenije] - **A unit, a department; a compartment**

Его отвезли в **отделение** реанимации. Надеюсь, врачам удастся спасти его жизнь.

They took him to the intensive care **unit**. Hopefully, the doctors will manage to save his life.

1579 - Волноваться [valna'vatsa] - *To worry*

Не нужно так **волноваться**. Есть много причин, по которым она может не брать трубку.

There's no need **to worry** so much. There are lots of reasons why she may not pick up the phone.

1580 - Нижний ['nizhnij] - *Lower, inferior*

На этой фотографии есть наш дедушка. Смотри, **нижний** ряд, первый справа.

There's our grandfather in this photo. Look, the **lower** row, the first on the right.

1581 - Штука ['shtuka] - **A thing (colloquial); a piece, an item**

Что это за странная **штука**? И почему она лежит у меня на кровати?

What kind of a strange **thing** is it? And why is it lying on my bed?

1582 - Защита [za'sthita] - *Protection, defense*

Защита вымирающих видов – это дело всей его жизни.

The **protection** of endangered species is a life work of his.

223

1583 - Вряд ли ['vrjadli] - *Unlikely, not likely, hardly*

Вряд ли это что-то серьёзное. Я думаю, ты просто простудился.

It's **unlikely** it is something serious. I think you've just caught a cold.

1584 - Выстрел ['vystrel] - *A shot, a gunshot*

Пожилая женщина сказала следователю, что слышала **выстрел** около семи часов вечера.

The elderly lady told the detective that she'd heard the **shot** at about seven p.m.

1585 - Тотчас ['totchas] - Immediately, at once (literary style)

Мы **тотчас** отправляем помощь! Оставайтесь на месте!

We're sending help **immediately**! Stay where you are!

1586 - Суть [sut'] - *Essence, gist*

Суть твоей идеи мне ясна. Но как мы реализуем её?

The **essence** of your idea is clear to me. But how are we going to realize it?

1587 - Труп [trup] - *A corpse, a dead body*

Детективы нашли **труп** в лесу, недалеко от дороги.

The detectives found the **corpse** in the forest, not far from the road.

1588 - Основа [as'nova] - *A basis, a foundation*

Любовь и понимание – это **основа** любых отношений.

Love and understanding is the **basis** of any relationship.

1589 - Подать [pa'dat'] - To give (perfective) (means to give something to someone who's far from the object)

Можешь **подать** мне ту большую книгу, которая рядом с тобой?

Can you **give** me the big book that's next to you?

1590 - Домашний [da'mashnij] - *Home-made; home (adj)*

Я удивлён! Этот консервированный суп на вкус почти как **домашний**.

I'm surprised! This canned soup tastes almost like a **home-made** one.

1591 - Готовить [ga'tovit'] - *To cook; to prepare*

Обычно я люблю **готовить**, но сегодня мне лень и я заказала пиццу.

Usually I like **to cook** but I'm lazy today and I've ordered some pizza.

1592 - Участие [u'tchastije] - *Participation*

Я не одобряю твоё **участие** в этом музыкальном конкурсе. Какая в нём польза?

I disapprove of your **participation** in this music contest. What's the use of it?

1593 - Жалеть [zha'let'] - *To regret, to be sorry*

Если ты не попробуешь сейчас, ты будешь **жалеть** об этом всю свою жизнь.

If you don't try now, you'll **regret** it all your life.

1594 - Фон [fon] - *A background*

Для этого яркого изображения мне нужен более нейтральный **фон**.

I need a more neutral **background** for this bright image.

1595 - Признак ['priznak] - *A sign, an indication*

Доктор сказал, что хороший аппетит – это **признак** выздоровления.

The doctor said that good appetite is **a sign** of recovery.

1596 - Врать [vrat'] - *To lie*

Не буду **врать**, мне всегда хотелось быть такой, как ты.

I won't **lie**, I've always wanted to be like you.

1597 - Возразить [vazra'zit'] - *To object, to mind, to protest*

Девушка хотела **возразить**, но шум заглушил её голос.

The girl wanted **to object** but the noise silenced her voice.

1598 - Дача ['datcha] - *A country house*

У нас есть **дача**, но она далеко от города.

We have **a country house** but it's far from the city.

1599 - Обо ['obə] - *About (a variation of preposition 'o' used before consonant clusters)*

Ты ничего не знаешь **обо** мне!

You know nothing **about** me!

1600 - Довольный [da'vol'nyj] - *Satisfied, pleased*

После ужина **довольный** кот мирно уснул у меня на коленях.

After supper the **satisfied** cat peacefully fell asleep on my lap.

1601 - Готовиться [ga'tovitsa] - *To get ready, to prepare oneself*

Завтра я буду **готовиться** к экзаменам и не смогу пойти с тобой по магазинам.

I'm going **to get ready** for my exams tomorrow and won't be able to go shopping with you.

1602 - Слой [sloj] - *A layer*

Перед покраской мы удалили толстый **слой** ржавчины.
Before painting we removed a thick **layer** of rust.

1603 - Охрана [ah'rana] - Security, guard, protection

Охрана супермаркета задержала магазинного воришку.
The supermarket **security** detained a shoplifter.

1604 - Превратиться [prevra'titsa] - *To turn into (intransitive)*

Иногда я хочу **превратиться** в птицу и улететь далеко отсюда.
Sometimes I want **to turn into** a bird and fly far away from here.

1605 - Милиционер [militsia'ner] - *A policeman, a militiaman*

За спасение ребёнка **милиционер** был награжден медалью.
The **policeman** was awarded a medal for saving a child.

1606 - Портрет [par'tret] - *A portrait*

Этот прекрасный **портрет** выставлен в музее, но никто не знает, кто его написал.
This wonderful **portrait** is displayed in the museum but nobody knows who painted it.

1607 - Терпеть [ter'pet'] - To endure, to stand, to tolerate

Зачем **терпеть** боль, если ты можешь принять таблетку?
Why **endure** the pain if you can take a pill?

1608 - Махнуть [mah'nut'] - To wave; to swap (colloquial)

Я попросил его **махнуть** рукой, когда он будет готов.
I asked him **to wave** his hand when he's ready.

1609 - Шкаф [shkaf] - *A wardrobe, a closet*

Если ты продолжишь покупать столько одежды, нам придётся купить ещё один **шкаф**.

If you go on buying so many clothes, we'll have to buy one more **wardrobe**.

1610 - Вес [ves] - *Weight*

Избыточный **вес** опасен для сердца.

Excessive **weight** is dangerous for the heart.

1611 - Холод ['holəd] - *Cold (low temperature)*

Я люблю зимний **холод**. Если он умеренный, конечно.

I like winter **cold**. If it's moderate, of course.

1612 - Определить [aprede'lit'] - *To determine, to define, to identify (perfective)*

Сложно **определить** точное количество жертв землетрясения.

It's hard **to determine** the exact number of earthquake victims.

1613 - Выпустить ['vypustit'] - *To release; to produce, to issue*

Постарайся **выпустить** плохую энергию и сконцентрируйся на хорошем.

Try **to release** bad energy and concentrate on the good things.

1614 - Тревога [tre'voga] - *Alarm, alert; anxiety*

Прошлой ночью пожарная **тревога** разбудила весь район, но она спасла много жизней.

Last night the fire **alarm** woke the whole neighborhood up but it saved lots of lives.

1615 - Выступать [vystu'pat'] - *To perform (on the stage)*

Завтра моя любимая группа будет **выступать** в центральном концертном зале.

Tomorrow my favorite band will **perform** in the central concert hall.

1616 - Полок ['polək] - Shelves (genitive plural)

Зачем тебе столько книжных **полок**? Насколько я знаю, ты не большой фанат чтения.

Why do you need so many book **shelves**? As far as I know, you're not a great fan of reading.

1617 - Куртка ['kurtka] - *A jacket*

Тебе нужна **куртка** потеплее. Эта слишком тонкая.

You need a warmer **jacket**. This one is too thin.

1618 - Спустя [spus'tja] - *Later, after*

Два года **спустя** я вернулся на то место, где посадил молодые деревья.

Two years **later** I returned to the place where I'd planted young trees.

1619 - Отчего [atche'vo] - Why (because of what reason; more often in literary style)

Отчего ты такой грустный сегодня? Что-то не так на работе?

Why are you so sad today? Anything wrong at work?

1620 - Изба [iz'ba] - A peasant's hut (archaic, used in modern language to ironically call a house or in set expressions like the one in the example that is literally translated as 'To take out dirt from one's house)

Зачем **выносить сор из избы**? Давай обсудим всё лично.

Why **wash our dirty linen in public**? Let's discuss everything in private.

1621 - Редко ['retkə] - *Rarely, seldom*

Я **редко** ем фастфуд, но вчера решила себя побаловать.
I **rarely** eat fast food but yesterday I decided to indulge myself.

1622 - Вершина [ver'shina] - *A peak, a summit*

Эта горная **вершина** не тает зимой, и она очень популярна среди туристов.
This mountain **peak** doesn't melt in winter and is very popular among tourists.

1623 - Тайный ['tajnyj] - *Secret (adj)*

Историки говорят, что под зданием есть **тайный** ход.
Historians say that there's a **secret** passage under the building.

1624 - Занятый ['zanjatyj] - *Engaged; occupied*

Водитель, **занятый** телефонным разговором, не заметил пешехода.
The driver **engaged** in a phone call didn't notice the pedestrian.

1625 - Рассматривать [rass'matrivat'] - *To consider, to address*

Неправильно **рассматривать** конфликт только с одной точки зрения.
It's not right **to consider** a conflict from only one point of view.

1626 - Отойти [ataj'ti] - *To move aside (perfective)*

Я выхожу на следующей остановке. Могу я попросить вас **отойти** немного?
I'm getting off at the next stop. May I ask you **to move aside** a bit?

1627 - Вырасти ['vyrasti] - To grow, to increase (perfective)

Эта должность дала мне возможность **вырасти** профессионально.

That position gave me an opportunity **to grow** professionally.

1628 - Париж [pa'rizh] - *Paris*

На наш медовый месяц мы поехали в **Париж**.
We went to **Paris** on our honeymoon.

1629 - Убийство [u'bijstvə] - *A murder*

Никто не знает, кто совершил это **убийство**, но есть несколько подозреваемых.

Nobody knows who committed this **murder** but there are a few suspects.

1630 - Рубашка [ru'bashka] - *A shirt*

Зачем тебе ещё одна **рубашка**? Мне кажется, у тебя их тысячи.

Why do you need another **shirt**? It seems to me you've got thousands of them.

1631 - Ox [oh] - Oh (mostly to express sadness or tiredness)

Ох, как я устала! А сегодня ещё только понедельник.
Oh, how tired I am! And it's only Monday today.

1632 - Хозяйство [ha'zjastvə] - *A household; economy; a farm*

Вести **хозяйство** и воспитывать детей не так просто, как кажется.

Maintaining the **household** and bringing up children is not as easy as it seems.

1633 - Парк [park] - *A park*

Парк вокруг дворца знаменит редкими видами деревьев и цветов.

The **park** around the palace is famous for the rare species of trees and flowers.

1634 - Перевести [pereves'ti] - *To translate, to interpret; to transfer (perfective)*

Я не смогу **перевести** этот текст без словаря.

I won't be able **to translate** this text without a dictionary.

1635 - Режим [re'zhim] - *A mode; a regime*

Переключись на спящий **режим**, если хочешь сэкономить заряд батареи.

Turn to sleep **mode** if you want to save the battery power.

1636 - Руководство [ruka'vodstvə] - *A guide, an instruction; leadership*

Перед использованием прибора внимательно прочитайте **руководство** пользователя.

Before using the appliance read the user **guide** attentively.

1637 - Посадить [pasa'dit'] - *To plant; to put to jail*

Я хочу **посадить** перед домом много деревьев, чтобы у меня был свой сад.

I want **to plant** lots of trees in front of my house to have my own garden.

1638 - Преступление [prestup'lenije] - *A crime*

Это **преступление** заслуживает самого жестокого наказания.

This **crime** deserves the most severe punishment.

1639 - Стенка ['stenka] - A side (of a container); a wall (diminutive of 'стена');

Нижняя **стенка** резервуара должна быть сделана из водонепроницаемого материала.

The lower **side** of the reservoir must be made of a waterproof material.

1640 - Орать [a'rat'] - *To yell, to scream*

Зачем так **орать**? Успокойся и объясни всё ещё раз.

Why **yell** so much? Calm down and explain everything once again.

1641 - Кругом [kru'gom] - *Around, round*

Кругом было так много сладостей и угощений, что я не знала, что выбрать.

There were so many sweets and treats around that I didn't know what to choose.

1642 - Обойтись [abaj'tis'] - *To do without (perfective)*

Мы не сможем **обойтись** без дополнительной помощи. У нас слишком мало опыта.

We won't be able **to do it without** extra help. We've got too little experience.

1643 - Луна [lu'na] - *The moon*

Луна спряталась за облаками, и стало совсем темно.
The moon hid behind the clouds and it got completely dark.

1644 - Богатый [ba'gatyj] - *Rich; a rich man*

Неужели он настолько **богатый**, что у него есть собственный самолёт?
Is he really so **rich** that he has his own airplane?

1645 - Гостиница [gas'tinitsa] - *A hotel, an inn*

Мне нравится эта **гостиница**: хороший сервис, доступная цена.

I like this **hotel**: good service, an affordable price.

1646 - Беседа [be'seda] - *A talk, a conversation*

Иногда всё, что нужно, – это душевная **беседа** за чашечкой чая.

Sometimes all you need is a soulful **talk** over a cup of tea.

1647 - Твёрдый ['tvjordyj] - *Firm, solid*

В темноте я споткнулась о какой-то **твёрдый** предмет и упала.

In the darkness I stumbled over some **firm** object and fell.

1648 - Полк [polk] - *A regiment (military)*

Когда солдат восстановился после ранения, он вернулся в **полк**.

When the soldier recovered from the wound he returned to the **regiment**.

1649 - Выдать ['vydat'] - *To give out*

Как ты мог **выдать** мой секрет? Ты обещал, что никому не скажешь!

How could you **give out** my secret? You promised you wouldn't tell anyone!

1650 - Лапа ['lapa] - *A paw*

Лапа этого огромного пса больше твоей руки!

The **paw** of this huge dog is bigger than your hand!

1651 - Воевать [vaje'vat'] - *To be at war, to wage war*

Я не хочу **воевать** с тобой. Давай попробуем помириться.

I don't want **to be at war** with you. Let's try to make up.

1652 - Останавливаться [asta'navlivatsa] - *To stop (reflexive)*

Мы уже сделали так много, и глупо **останавливаться** сейчас.

We've already done so much, and it's silly **to stop** now.

1653 - Никуда [niku'da] - *(To) nowhere*

У неё ужасная депрессия. Она **никуда** не ходит и ни с кем не общается.

She's got a terrible depression. She goes **nowhere** and doesn't communicate with anyone.

1654 - Обладать [abla'dat'] - *To possess, to own*

Нужно **обладать** огромным терпением, чтобы жить с таким человеком, как твой муж.

One must **possess** enormous patience to live with a person like your husband.

1655 - Продать [pra'dat'] - *To sell (perfective)*

Извините, но я не могу **продать** эти часы. Это семейная реликвия.

Sorry, but I can't **sell** this watch. It's a family heirloom.

1656 - Спорить ['sporit'] - *To dispute, to argue*

Даже не пытайся **спорить** с ним. Его невозможно переубедить.

Don't even try **to dispute** with him. It's impossible to dissuade him.

1657 - Солнечный ['solnetchnyj] - *Sunny*

Жаль, что тебе приходится оставаться дома в такой **солнечный** день.

It's a pity you have to stay at home on such a **sunny** day.

1658 - Забор [za'bor] - *A fence*

Между нашими домами стоит **высокий** забор. Жизнь соседей меня совсем не интересует.

There's a high **fence** between our houses. I'm not interested in my neighbors' life at all.

1659 - Больший ['bol'shij] - *Greater, bigger, larger*

Мой сын проявляет **больший** интерес к книгам, чем к спорту.

My son shows **greater** interest in books than in sports.

1660 - Пост [post] - *A post, a position*

Маргарет Тэтчер занимала **пост** премьер-министра двенадцать лет.

Margaret Thatcher held the **post** of Prime Minister for twelve years.

1661 - Полезть [pa'lest'] - *To climb (perfective)*

Нужно быть сумасшедшим, чтобы **полезть** на такую высокую гору в одиночку.

One must be crazy **to climb** such a high mountain alone.

1662 - Печальный [pe'tchal'nyj] - *Sorrowful, grieved*

В последнее время у неё такой **печальный** вид, будто кто-то умер.

She's had such a **sorrowful** look recently, as if someone died.

1663 - Выполнять [vypal'njat'] - *To carry out, to fulfill*

Пока моя коллега в отпуске, я буду **выполнять** её обязанности.

While my colleague is on holiday I'll be **carrying out** her duties.

1664 - Требоваться ['trebavatsa] - *To be required, to be needed*

Для должной организации мероприятия будет **требоваться** много усилий.

Much effort will **be required** for proper organisation of the event.

1665 - Бледный ['blednyj] - *Pale*

Почему ты такой **бледный**? Ты что, увидел привидение?

Why are you so **pale**? Have you seen a ghost?

1666 - Умирать [umi'rat'] - *To die*

Никто не хочет **умирать**, особенно в таком молодом возрасте.

Nobody wants **to die**, especially at such a young age.

1667 - Шапка ['shapka] - A hat (a warm piece of clothing, without brims)

Эта шерстяная **шапка** тёплая, но очень колючая.

This woolen **hat** is warm but very itchy.

1668 - Дойти [daj'ti] - *To walk to, to reach*

До вокзала можно **дойти** за десять минут. Зачем садиться на автобус?

One can **walk** to the railway station in ten minutes. Why take a bus?

1669 - Успокоиться [uspa'koitsa] - *To calm down*

Мне нужно немного побыть одной, чтобы **успокоиться**. Оставьте меня.

I need to be alone for some time **to calm down**. Leave me.

1670 - Университет [universi'tet] - *A university*

В **университет** поступить не просто, но это того стоит.

It's not easy to enter **a university** but it's worth it.

1671 - Бабка ['babka] - An old woman (colloquial, mostly scornfully)

Та **бабка**, которая живёт на втором этаже, снова пыталась учить меня жизни!

That **old woman** who lives on the second floor tried to teach me about life again!

1672 - Журналист [zhurna'list] - *A journalist*

Этот **журналист** имеет своё мнение обо всех событиях. Я люблю читать его колонку.

This **journalist** has his own opinion about all the events. I like reading his column.

1673 - Должность ['dolzhnast'] - *A position, a post*

Он так сильно хотел эту **должность**, что был готов врать и унижаться.

He wanted that **position** so much that he was ready to lie and grovel.

1674 - Приближаться [pribli'zhatsa] - *To approach, to near*

Разбуди меня, когда мы начнём **приближаться** к нашей станции.

Wake me up when we start **approaching** our station.

1675 - Истина ['istina] - *Verity, truth*

Правда и **истина** – это разные вещи. Ты согласен?

Truth and **verity** are different things. Do you agree?

1676 - Раствор [rast'vor] - *Solution*

Я оставила свой **раствор** для контактных линз дома. Ты можешь одолжить мне свой?

I left my contact lens **solution** at home. Can you lend me yours?

1677 - Газ [gas] - *Gas*

Этот **газ** очень токсичен. Обращайтесь с ним осторожно.
This **gas** is very toxic. Handle it with care.

1678 - Позиция [pa'zitsija] - *A position, an attitude*

Твоя **позиция** по этому вопросу мне не ясна. Почему ты против?
Your **position** on this matter is not clear to me. Why are you against it?

1679 - Летать [le'tat'] - *To fly*

Этот птенец ещё не умеет **летать** и полностью зависит от родителей.
This nestling can't **fly** yet and depends entirely on its parents.

1680 - Неожиданный [nea'zhydannyj] - *Unexpected, sudden*

Её **неожиданный** приезд всех нас приятно удивил.
Her **unexpected** arrival pleasantly surprised us all.

1681 - Убивать [ubi'vat'] - *To kill, to murder*

Курение продолжает **убивать** тысячи людей по всему миру.
Smoking is continuing **to kill** thousands of people all over the world.

1682 - Появление [pajav'lenije] - *Appearance, emergence*

Я никогда не забуду своё первое **появление** в новостях.
I'll never forget my first **appearance** in the news.

1683 - Глухой [glu'hoj] - *Deaf*

Я не **глухой**. Не обязательно говорить так громко.
I'm not **deaf**. It's not necessary to talk so loudly.

1684 - Обыкновенный [abykna'vennyj] - *Usual, ordinary*

Это был **обыкновенный** скучный рабочий день и я не ожидал никаких сюрпризов.

That was an **ordinary** boring working day and I wasn't expecting any surprises.

1685 - Двинуться ['dvinutsa] - To move (intransitive, perfective, means to start moving)

Я так устал, что не могу **двинуться** с места.
I'm so tired that I can't **move**.

1686 - Решительный [re'shitel'nyj] - *Decisive, resolute*

Что мне больше всего нравится в нём, так это то, что он **решительный** и никогда не сомневается.

What I like about him most of all is that he's **decisive** and never has doubts.

1687 - Спуститься [spust'titsa] - To go down, to decsend (perfective)

Она обещала **спуститься** к ужину. Сходи проверь, что она делает.

She promised **to come down** for supper. Go check what she's doing.

1688 - Песнь [pesn'] - A song (archaic or poetic)

О, **песнь** соловья так романтична!
Oh, the nightingale's **song** is so romantic!

1689 - Облако ['oblakə] - *A cloud*

Это белое **облако** напоминает котёнка, играющего с мячиком.
This white **cloud** resembles a kitten playing with a ball.

1690 - Морда ['morda] - A muzzle; a face (colloquial, rude or ironic)

Морда твоей собаки вся покрыта паутиной. Где она была?
Your dog's **muzzle** is all covered in spider web. Where has it been?

1691 - Записка [za'piska] - *A note*

Где **записка**, которую оставила мама? Там написано, что мы должны сделать по дому.
Where's the **note** that mom left? It says what we must do around the house.

1692 - Иностранный [ina'strannyj] - *Foreign*

Изучая **иностранный** язык, также важно узнавать об особенностях культуры.
While studying a **foreign** language it's also important to learn the peculiarities of the culture.

1693 - Незнакомый [nezna'komyj] - *Unfamiliar, unknown*

Заходил какой-то **незнакомый** человек и сказал, что хочет поговорить с тобой.
Some **unfamiliar** man dropped by and said he wanted to talk to you.

1694 - Устоновить [ustana'vit'] - *To install, to mount*

Я скачал новую программу, но не знаю, как её **установить**.
I've downloaded a new software program but I don't know how **to install** it.

1695 - Забывать [zaby'vat'] - *To forget*

Мы не должны **забывать** тех, кто отдал свои жизни ради нашей свободы.

We shouldn't **forget** those who gave their lives for the sake of our freedom.

1696 - Позвать [paz'vat'] - *To call; to invite*

Можешь **позвать** сестру и сказать, что завтрак готов?

Can you **call** your sister and tell her the breakfast is ready?

1697 - Физический [fi'zitcheskij] - *Physical, bodily; physics (adj)*

Иногда психологический ущерб может иметь более серьёзные последствия, чем **физический**.

Sometimes moral harm can have more serious consequences than **physical** harm.

1698 - Ус [us] - Most often used in plural 'Усы - [u'sy]' - Moustache

Сбрей свои **усы**. С ними ты выглядишь гораздо старше.

Shave your **moustache** off. You look much older with it.

1699 - Помещение [pame'stchenije] - A room, a premise (as an opposite to outdoors)

Не забывай снимать шляпу, когда входишь в **помещение**.

Don't forget to take your hat off when entering a **room**.

1700 - Испугаться [ispu'gatsa] - To get frightened, to get scared (perfective)

Твой костюм Дракулы выглядит так реалистично, что можно **испугаться**.

Your Dracula costume looks so realistic that one can **get frightened**.

1701 - Плащ [plastch] - *A raincoat, an overcoat*

Этот **плащ** идеален для дождливой погоды. Он водонепроницаемый и достаточно тёплый.
This **raincoat** is perfect for rainy weather. It's waterproof and warm enough.

1702 - Еле ['jele] - Barely, hardly, scarcely

Когда спасатели вытащили его из воды, он **еле** дышал.
When the rescuers pulled him out of the water he was **barely** breathing.

1703 - Темно [tem'no] - *Dark (adv)*

Уже становится **темно**. Нам лучше пойти домой, иначе мама будет волноваться.
It's getting **dark** already. We'd better go home otherwise Mom will be worried.

1704 - Подъезд [pad'jezd] - Entrance (the main one, most often in a block of flats)

Мой **подъезд** первый от супермаркета. Номер квартиры ты помнишь?
My **entrance** is the first one from the supermarket. Do you remember the apartment number?

1705 - Съесть [sjest'] - To eat, to eat up (perfective)

Я такой голодный, что могу **съесть** целого слона!
I'm so hungry I could **eat** a whole elephant!

1706 - Прочесть [pra'tchest'] - To read (completely), to read through (perfective)

Я не смогла **прочесть** все книги из списка, который учитель задал нам на лето.

I didn't manage **to read** all the books from the list the teacher assigned us for summer.

1707 - Следователь ['sledavatel'] - *An investigator, a detective*

Следователь допросил всех свидетелей и записал все детали в блокнот.

The **investigator** interrogated all the witnesses and put down all the details in a notebook.

1708 - Двенадцать [dve'nadtsat'] - *Twelve*

Когда часы пробьют **двенадцать**, карета снова превратится в тыкву.

When the clock strikes **twelve** the carriage will turn into a pumpkin again.

1709 - Задуматься [za'dumatsa] - To think (means to begin to think), to reflect

Тебе пора **задуматься** о том, чтобы завести детей.

It's time for you **to think** about having children.

1710 - Решать [re'shat'] - *To solve, to sort out*

Ты не обязана **решать** эту проблему в одиночку. У тебя есть мы.

You don't have **to solve** this problem alone. You have us.

1711 - Особенный [a'sobennyj] - *Special*

Я хочу найти для неё **особенный** подарок. Она заслуживает самого лучшего.

I want to find a **special** present for her. She deserves the best.

1712 - Подарить [pada'rit'] - *To give, to present*

Я не знаю, что **подарить** родителям на годовщину свадьбы.
I don't know what **to give** my parents for their wedding anniversary.

1713 - Измениться [izme'nitsa] - To change (intransitive, perfective)

Мы планируем приехать в августе, но наши планы могут **измениться**.
We're planning to come in August, but our plans can **change**.

1714 - Платок [pla'tok] - *A handkerchief; a shawl*

Я положила чистый **платок** в правый карман твоих брюк.
I put a clean **handkerchief** into the right pocket of your trousers.

1715 - Мощный ['mostchnyj] - *Powerful*

Мощный взрыв уничтожил практически всё здание.
The **powerful** explosion destroyed almost all the building.

1716 - Середина [sere'dina] - *A middle*

Сейчас **середина** месяца, а я уже потратил все деньги.
It's the **middle** of the month now and I've already spent all the money.

1717 - Сумасшедший [suma'shedshij] - *Crazy, mad; a madman*

Ты что, **сумасшедший**? Как ты можешь ехать на такой скорости?
Are you **crazy**? How can you drive at such a speed?

1718 - Наверняка [navern'ə'ka] - *For sure, certainly*

Я думаю, что сдал тест, но узнаю **наверняка** только после того, как опубликуют результаты.

I think I passed the test but I'll know **for sure** only when they publish the results.

1719 - Здорово ['zdoravə] - *Great, awesome*

Должно быть, **здорово** путешествовать так много, как твой одногруппник.

That must be **great** to travel as much as your groupmate does.

1720 - Напряжение [napr'ə'zhenije] - *Tension; voltage*

Между ними всегда присутствовало некоторое **напряжение** из-за того, что они раньше встречались.

There was always some **tension** between them, because they used to date.

1721 - Могила [ma'gila] - *A grave*

Эта **могила** всегда покрыта свежими цветами. Кто здесь похоронен?

This **grave** is always covered with fresh flowers. Who's been buried here?

1722 - Тоска [tas'ka] - *Melancholy, boredom, sadness*

Твоя **тоска** убивает тебя! Приободрись и начни действовать!

Your **melancholy** is killing you! Cheer up and start acting!

1723 - Приводить [priva'dit'] - *To bring (with); to lead (to), to result in*

Нельзя **приводить** с собой на праздник людей, не спросив хозяина.

One can't **bring** people to a party with them without asking the host.

1724 - Удивляться [udiv'l'atsa] - *To be surprised, to wonder (at)*

Не стоит **удивляться**, что она такая эгоистичная. Она единственный ребёнок в семье.

One shouldn't **be surprised** that she's so selfish. She's an only child in the family.

1725 - Буквально [buk'val'nə] - *Literally*

Это займёт **буквально** две минуты. Вам не придётся ждать.

It'll take **literally** two minutes. You won't have to wait.

1726 - Борт [bort] - *A board (about a ship or a plane); a side*

Капитан разрешил нам взойти на **борт** и прогуляться по кораблю.

The captain allowed us to get on **board** and to have a walk about the ship.

1727 - Забрать [zab'rat'] - *To take away*

Есть вещи, которые никто не сможет у нас **забрать**. Например, любовь и вера.

There are things that nobody can **take away** from us. Love and faith, for example.

1728 - Грех [greh] - *A sin*

Самоубийство – единственный **грех**, который Бог не прощает.

Suicide is the only **sin** that God doesn't forgive.

1729 - Несчастный [ne'shchasnyj] - *Unhappy, miserable; unlucky*

Кто сказал, что он **несчастный** человек? Он просто не умеет ценить то, что имеет.

Who said he's an **unhappy** person? He just can't appreciate what he has.

1730 - Строй [stroj] - A system, an order, a regime

Политический **строй** этой страны основан на тирании и насилии.

The political **system** of this country is based on tyranny and violence.

1731 - Занять [za'n'at'] - *To take (about time)*

Полная реконструкция здания должна **занять** около трёх месяцев.

The complete reconstruction of the building will **take** about three months.

1732 - Исследование [iss'ledavanije] - *Research*

Научное **исследование** профессора длилось более десяти лет и принесло поразительные результаты.

The professor's scientific **research** lasted more than ten years and brought amazing results.

1733 - Доказать [daka'zat'] - *To prove*

Мы сможем **доказать**, что ты невиновен, только если ты будешь говорить правду.

We'll be able **to prove** that you're innocent only if you tell the truth.

1734 - Буква ['bukva] - *A letter (alphabet)*

Какая первая **буква** русского алфавита?
What's the first **letter** of the Russian alphabet?

1735 - Реакция [re'aktsija] - *A reaction, a response*

Реакция общества на теракт была однозначной.
The **reaction** of the society to the terrorist act was unambiguous.

1736 - Варить [va'rit'] - *To boil, to cook*

Эти креветки не нужно **варить**. Просто положи их в горячую воду.

There's no need **to boil** the shrimps. Just put them into hot water.

1737 - Мужской [muzhs'koj] - *Male, masculine; man's, gentleman's*

Я услышала незнакомый **мужской** голос внизу и спустилась проверить, кто это.

I heard an unfamiliar **male** voice downstairs and went down to check who it was.

1738 - Резкий ['reskij] - *Sharp, abrupt*

Резкий спад экономического роста сильно повлиял на зарплаты.

The **sharp** decline of the economic growth affected the salaries badly.

1739 - Пила [pi'la] - *A saw*

Пила застряла в стволе дерева, и я не знаю, как вытащить её.

The **saw** is stuck in the tree trunk and I don't know how to get it out.

1740 - Литературный [litera'turnyj] - *Literary*

Твой **литературный** стиль неуместен в наших повседневных разговорах.

Your **literary** style is out of place in our everyday talks.

1741 - Изменить [izme'nit'] - *To change (perfective)*

Мы ничего не можем **изменить** в этой ситуации. Мы можем только ждать.

We can't **change** anything in this situation. We can only wait.

1742 - Обезьяна [abez'jana] - *A monkey*

В цирке **обезьяна** украла мой кошелёк, пока я пытался сфотографироваться с ней.

In the circus **a monkey** stole my purse while I was trying to take a photo with it.

1743 - Бригада [bri'gada] - A team, a crew (a group of people employed to work together on a task)

Строительная **бригада** должна закончить дом к середине ноября, если погода позволит.

The construction **team** will have to finish the house by the middle of November if the weather permits.

1744 - Ловить [la'vit'] - *To catch*

Лягушки могут **ловить** насекомых своими длинными языками.

Frogs can **catch** insects with their long tongues.

1745 - Остаток [as'tatək] - A remainder, the rest; a surplus

Я хочу провести **остаток** отпуска на даче без суеты и шума.

I want to spend the **remainder** of my holiday in the country house without any fuss and noise.

1746 - Стремиться [stre'mitsa] - *To strive, to aspire*

Для человека естественно **стремиться** стать лучше.

It's natural for a human being **to strive** for becoming better.

1747 - Пункт [punkt] - *A point; a station*

Этот **пункт** твоей презентации лучше заменить чем-то другим.

It's better to replace this **point** of your presentation with something else.

1748 - Тянуться [t'ə'nutsa] - *To drag on*

Я никогда не думал, что время может **тянуться** так долго.
I've never thought time could **drag on** for so long.

1749 - Локоть ['lokat'] - *An elbow*

Удивительно, но ни один человек не может укусить свой **локоть**.
It's amazing but no man can bite his own **elbow**.

1750 - Обязанный [a'b'azannyj] - *Obliged*

Продавец, **обязанный** принять бракованный товар, отказался это сделать.
The seller, **obliged** to accept the faulty good, refused to do it.

1751 - Краска ['kraska] - *Paint, dye*

Краска на этой чашке уже поцарапалась, но она всё равно моя любимая.
The **paint** on this cup is scratched already but still it's my favorite one.

1752 - Разница ['raznitsa] - *A difference*

Разница в возрасте никак не влияет на нашу дружбу.
The age **difference** doesn't affect our friendship in any way.

1753 - Расстояние [rasta'janije] - *A distance*

Это **расстояние** слишком большое для меня. Я не привыкла столько ходить пешком.
This **distance** is too long for me. I'm not used to walking on foot so much.

1754 - Кружок [kru'zhok] - An interest group; a circle (small)

Мой сын посещает художественный **кружок** после уроков.
After classes my son attends an art **interest group**.

1755 - Пожилой [pazhi'loj] - *Elderly*

Пожилой мужчина попросил меня объяснить ему, как пользоваться банкоматом.
An **elderly** man asked me to explain to him how to use a cash machine.

1756 - Непонятно [nepa'njatnə] - It is unclear (impersonal); incomprehensively

Мне **непонятно**, почему женщинам часто платят меньше, чем мужчинам.
It is unclear to me why women are often paid less than men.

1757 - Окончательно [akan'tchatel'nə] - *Finally, definitevely*

Мы опубликуем только **окончательно** утверждённый текст статьи.
We'll publish only the **finally** approved text of the article.

1758 - Дон [don] - *The Don River*

Дон протекает в европейской части России.
The Don River flows through the European part of Russia.

1759 - Заставлять [zastav'l'at'] - *To make, to force*

Зачем **заставлять** ребёнка есть суп, если он не хочет?
Why **make** the child eat soup if he doesn't want to?

1760 - Удивительный [udi'vitel'nyj] - *Amazing, marvelous, wonderful*

Поздравляю тебя с днём рождения! Ты **удивительный** человек, и я рад, что ты есть в моей жизни.

Happy birthday to you! You're an **amazing** person and I'm glad I have you.

1761 - Страдать [stra'dat'] - *To suffer*

Посевы продолжают **страдать** от засухи.

The crops are continuing **to suffer** from drought.

1762 - Седой [se'doj] - *Grey-haired, grey*

Ты всё принимаешь близко к сердцу, поэтому ты уже **седой**. А ты ещё такой молодой!

You take everything close to heart which is why you're **grey-haired** already. And you're still so young!

1763 - Политика [pa'litika] - *A policy; politics*

Новая экономическая **политика** обещает большие перемены.

The new economic **policy** promises great changes.

1764 - Поколение [paka'lenije] - *A generation*

Каждое новое **поколение** думает, что оно лучше остальных.

Every new **generation** think they're better than the one before.

1765 - Ожидание [azhi'danije] - *Waiting, expectation*

Ожидание хуже всего на свете: ты ничего не можешь сделать, и от тебя ничего не зависит.

Waiting is worse than anything else in the world: you can't do anything, and nothing depends on you.

1766 - Записать [zapi'sat'] - To write down; to register, to enroll

У тебя есть лист бумаги и ручка? Я хочу **записать** этот рецепт.
Have you got a sheet of paper and a pen? I want **to write down** this recipe.

1767 - Фонарь [fa'nar'] - *A lamppost; a lantern*

Этот **фонарь** у моего дома такой яркий! Он мешает мне уснуть по ночам.
This **lamppost** by my house is so bright! It prevents me from sleeping at night.

1768 - Куча ['kutcha] - *A pile, a heap*

Эта **куча** бумаг на твоём столе с каждым днём становится всё больше и больше!
This **pile** of papers on your desk is getting bigger and bigger every day!

1769 - Полоса [pala'sa] - *A streak, a strip*

Надеюсь, теперь **полоса** неудач в моей жизни закончилась.
I hope the **streak** of bad luck in my life is over now.

1770 - Страсть [strast'] - *A passion*

Пение это не просто её хобби, это её **страсть**.
Singing is not just a hobby of hers, it's her **passion**.

1771 - Сержант [ser'zhant] - *A sergeant (military)*

Этот молодой **сержант** полиции помогает мне с расследованием.
This young police **sergeant** is helping me with the investigation.

1772 - Святой [sv'ə'toj] - *A saint; saint*

Этот **святой** считается покровителем торговли.
This **saint** is considered to be the patron of trade.

1773 - Повесть ['povest'] - A story, a tale (a genre of narrative, something between a short story and a novel in size)

Эта **повесть** рассказывает о неразделённой любви.
This **story** tells about unanswered love.

1774 - Шёпот ['shopət] - *A whisper*

Я слышала тихий **шёпот** в соседней комнате, но не смогла разобрать, кто говорит.
I heard a quiet **whisper** in the next room but couldn't make out who was talking.

1775 - Теория [te'orija] - *A theory*

Его **теория** основана на многолетних исследованиях.
His **theory** is based on longstanding research.

1776 - Интересовать [interesa'vat'] - *To interest, to concern*

Почему меня должна **интересовать** твоя личная жизнь?
Why should your personal life **interest** me?

1777 - Чисто [tchis'tə] - Clean (adv or impersonal), neatly

Дома так **чисто**! Когда вы успели всё убрать?
The house is so **clean**! When did you have time to tidy everything up?

1778 - Пояс ['pojas] - *A belt*

Тонкий кожаный **пояс** красиво подчёркивал её талию.
A thin leather **belt** circled her waist beautifully.

1779 - Близко ['blizkə] - Close (adv) (both figuratively and literally), near

Мы жили **близко** друг к другу и провели всё детство вместе.
We used to live **close** to each other and spent our whole childhood together.

1780 - Включить [vklu'tchit'] - To turn on; to include (perfective)

Уже пора **включить** свет. Я не вижу, что читаю.
It's time **to turn on** the light. I don't see what I'm reading.

1781 - Поразить [para'zit'] - To strike, to amaze; to strike, to hit

Её талант просто не мог не **поразить** жюри.
Her talent just couldn't but **strike** the jury.

1782 - Вокзал [vak'zal'] - *A railway station*

Я отвезу тебя на **вокзал** и подожду, пока не прибудет твой поезд.
I'll take you to the **railway station** and wait until your train arrives.

1783 - Вещество [vestchest'vo] - *A substance, a matter*

Мы отправили **вещество** в лабораторию для более подробного анализа.
We sent the **substance** to the laboratory for a more detailed analysis.

1784 - Частный ['tchasnyj] - *Private*

Частный вертолёт президента приземлился за зданием парламента.
The president's **private** helicopter landed behind the Parliament building.

1785 - Корень ['koren'] - *A root*

Корень этого растения целебный. Его можно заваривать и пить как чай.

The **root** of this plant is healing. It can be infused and drunk as tea.

1786 - Помолчать [pamal'tchat'] - To keep silent, to be silent (for a while)

Дети, неужели вы не можете **помолчать** хотя бы минуту?

Kids, can't you really **keep silent** for at least a minute?

1787 - Столовый [sta'lovyj] - *Table (adj)*

Этот столовый **сервиз** сделан из фарфора.

This **table** set is made of china.

1788 - Ткань [tkan'] - *A cloth*

Эта гладкая шёлковая **ткань** подойдёт для платья, которое я шью.

This smooth silk **cloth** will suit the dress I'm sewing.

1789 - Открыться [at'krytsa] - To open (reflexive, perfective); to confide

Новый аквапарк должен **открыться** через неделю.

The new water park must **open** in a week.

1790 - Поток [pa'tok] - *A torrent, a stream*

Горный **поток** заканчивался высоким водопадом.

The mountain **torrent** ended with a high waterfall.

1791 - Вынужденный ['vynuzhdennyj] - *Forced*

Вынужденный отъезд отца расстроил всю семью.

Father's **forced** departure upset the whole family.

1792 - Полиция [pa'litsija] - *Police*

Полиция не смогла предотвратить преступление.

The **police** was unable to avert the crime.

1793 - Стыдный ['stydnyj] - **Not used in the infinitive, the most widespread form is the impersonal one - стыдно [stydnə] - To be ashamed**

Я не понимаю, почему мне должно быть **стыдно** за то, что я сказала правду.

I don't understand why I should **be ashamed** of having told the truth.

1794 - База ['baza] - *A base*

Военная **база**, на которой работает мой отец, – секретный объект.

The military **base** my father works at is a secret location.

1795 - Слышно ['slyshnə] - *One can hear (impersonal)*

Отсюда мне хорошо **слышно**, что они говорят. Я могу разобрать каждое слово.

From here I **can hear** very well what they're saying. I can make out every single word.

1796 - Строгий ['strogij] - *Strict*

Её **строгий** вид – всего лишь маска. На самом деле она добрая и понимающая.

Her **strict** looks are just a mask. In reality she's kind and understanding.

1797 - Шинель [shi'nel'] - *A uniform overcoat (military)*

Шинель солдата промокла насквозь, и он боялся что может простудиться.

The soldier's **uniform overcoat** got wet through, and he was afraid he might catch a cold.

1798 - Блестящий [bles't'astchij] - *Brilliant; shining, glittering*

Твой дядя **блестящий** адвокат. Я впечатлен его знаниями!
Your uncle is a **brilliant** lawyer. I'm impressed by his knowledge!

1799 - Выбор ['vybor] - *A choice*

Я думаю, ты сделала правильный **выбор**. Семья важнее, чем деньги.
I think you've made the right **choice**. Family is more important than money.

1800 - Сведения ['svedenija] - *Information, intelligence*

Эти **сведения** из надёжного источника. Не сомневайся.
This **information** is from a reliable source. Have no doubts.

1801 - Комиссия [ka'misija] - *A commission, a committee*

Для проверки состояния завода была создана специальная **комиссия.**
A special **commission** was created to check the condition of the factory.

1802 - Направить [nap'ravit'] - *To direct*

Мы решили **направить** ваше дело в апелляционный суд.
We've decided **to direct** your case to the court of appeals.

1803 - Палка ['palka] - *A stick, a cane*

Мальчик притворился, что **палка** – это его винтовка.
The boy pretended his **stick** was his rifle.

1804 - Запомнить [za'pomnit'] - *To memorize*

Я не могу **запомнить** её имя и не знаю, как к ней обращаться.

I can't **memorize** her name and don't know how to address her.

1805 - Бороться [ba'rotsa] - *To fight, to struggle*

Тебе нужно **бороться** с твоей депрессией. Так не может больше продолжаться.

You need **to fight** with your depression. It can't go on like that anymore.

1806 - Везти [ves'ti] - To drive (to carry by vehicle); to be lucky

Мне пришлось самой **везти** детей в клинику, потому что муж был на работе.

I had **to drive** the children to the clinic myself because my husband was at work.

1807 - Колонна [ka'lona] - *A column, a pillar*

Высокая **колонна** в центре площади была воздвигнута в честь великой победы.

The tall **column** in the middle of the square was erected in honor of the great victory.

1808 - Лёд [ljod] - *Ice*

У нас есть **лёд** в холодильнике? Я хочу охладить свой напиток.

Do we have any **ice** in the fridge? I want to cool my drink.

1809 - Замечательный [zame'tchatel'nyj] - *Remarkable, outstanding*

В той ситуации ты проявил **замечательный** профессионализм.

You showed **remarkable** professionalism in that situation.

1810 - Надпись ['natpis'] - *An inscription*

Странная **надпись** на стене пещеры привлекла внимание многих учёных.

A strange **inscription** on the cave wall attracted the attention of many scientists.

1811 - Одинокий [adi'nokij] - *Lonely, lonesome*

У меня нет семьи, но я не могу сказать, что я **одинокий** человек.

I don't have a family but I can't say I'm a **lonely** person.

1812 - Пиджак [pid'zhak] - *A jacket (a suit jacket for men)*

На улице было холодно, и он любезно предложил ей свой **пиджак**.

It was cold outside and he kindly offered his **jacket to her**.

1813 - Тарелка [ta'relka] - *A plate*

Фарфоровая **тарелка** выскользнула из её рук и разбилась на сотни кусочков.

The china **plate** slipped out of her hands and broke into hundreds of pieces.

1814 - Научиться [nau'tchitsa] - *To learn*

Я хочу **научиться** играть на музыкальном инструменте. Например, на скрипке.

I want **to learn** how to play a musical instrument. The violin, for example.

1815 - Пища ['pistcha] - *Food*

Пища должна быть здоровой и сбалансированной.
Food must be healthy and balanced.

1816 - Назначить [naz'natchit'] - *To appoint, to designate*

Во вторник президент собирается **назначить** новых министров.

On Tuesday the president is going **to appoint** new ministers.

1817 - Подруга [pad'ruga] - *A friend (female)*

Моя лучшая **подруга** всегда знает, что мне нужно.

My best **friend** always knows what I need.

1818 - Выбирать [vybi'rat'] - *To choose, to select*

Она совсем не умеет **выбирать** одежду и часто выглядит нелепо.

She's absolutely unable **to choose** clothes and often looks ridiculous.

1819 - Взрыв [vzryv] - *An explosion*

Взрыв причинил огромный ущерб машинам, припаркованным перед зданием.

The **explosion** did enormous harm to the cars parked in front of the building.

1820 - Сущность ['sustchnəst'] - *Essence, nature*

В сложных обстоятельствах люди проявляют свою истинную **сущность**.

In hard circumstances people show their true **essence**.

1821 - Батарея [bata'reja] - *A battery (electrical); a radiator*

Она разговаривала по телефону всю ночь, пока не села **батарея**.

She was talking on the phone the whole night until the **battery** was out.

1822 - Техника ['tehnika] - An equipment, machinery; a technique

Это сложная **техника**. Боюсь, я не смогу её починить.
It's a complicated piece of **equipment**. I'm afraid I won't be able to fix it.

1823 - Пастух [pas'tuh] - *A shepherd*

Пастух уснул, и стадо разбежалось по всему полю.
The **shepherd** fell asleep and the herd scattered about the field.

1824 - Напомнить [na'pomnit'] - *To remind*

Не забудь **напомнить** мне поставить будильник.
Don't forget **to remind** me to set the alarm clock.

1825 - Сомневаться [samnə'vatsa] - *To doubt*

Не позволяй никому заставить тебя **сомневаться** в правильности своего решения.
Don't let anyone make you **doubt** the correctness of your decision.

1826 - Крыльцо [kryl''tso] - *A porch*

Будь осторожен! **Крыльцо** мокрое после дождя.
Be careful! The **porch** is wet after the rain.

1827 - Радоваться ['radavatsa] - *To rejoice, to be happy*

Способность **радоваться** за других людей – редкое явление в современном мире.
The ability **to rejoice** for other people is a rare phenomenon in the modern world.

1828 - Покрыть [pak'ryt'] - To cover (perfective) (both literally and figuratively)

Этой суммы не достаточно, чтобы **покрыть** все мои расходы.
This sum is not enough **to cover** all my expenses.

1829 - Глянуть ['gl'anut'] - To take a look, to glance (to have a brief look, often to check something)

Я подготовила все документы. Можешь **глянуть**.
I've prepared all the documents. You may **take a look**.

1830 - Значительный [zna'tchitel'nyj] - *Signififcant, considerable*

Эта организация внесла **значительный** вклад в культурное развитие страны.
This organisation made a **significant** contribution to the cultural development of the country.

1831 - Захватить [zahva'tit'] - To capture, to seize (perfective)

Во многих фильмах злодеи пытаются **захватить** весь мир.
In many movies villains are trying **to capture** the whole world.

1832 - Вождь [vosht'] - A chief (of a tribe), (often related to Soviet leaders)

Люди говорили, что Ленин – **вождь** революции.
People used to say that Lenin was the **chief** of the revolution.

1833 - Восточный [vas'tochnyj] - *Eastern*

Восточный мир полон особенных традиций, которые непонятны большинству европейцев.
The **eastern** world is full of special traditions that are unclear to most europeans.

1834 - Приносить [prina'sit'] - *To bring, to fetch*

Пока ты болеешь, я могу **приносить** тебе продукты, если хочешь.

While you're ill I can **bring** you some food, if you like.

1835 - Международный [mezhduna'rodnyj] - *International*

К счастью, **международный** конфликт был разрешен быстрее, чем ожидалось.

Luckily, the **international** conflict was resolved faster than expected.

1836 - Необходимость [neapha'dɪməst'] - *A necessity, a need*

Государство признаёт **необходимость** реформирования политической системы.

The state admits the **necessity** of reforming the political system.

1837 - Оттого [atta'vo] - *That is why*

Он первый раз в таком большом городе, **оттого** он немного смущён.

It's his first time in such a big city, **that is why** he's a bit embarrassed.

1838 - Духовный [du'hovnyj] - *Spiritual*

Этот священник – глубоко **духовный** человек, почти святой.

This priest is a deeply **spiritual** man, almost a saint.

1839 - Голод ['goləd] - *Hunger*

Голод в оккупированном городе заставлял людей забывать о своих ценностях.

The **hunger** in the occupied city made people forget about their values.

1840 - Девица [de'vitsa] - *A damsel, a maid*

Девица, попавшая в беду, – классический сюжет многих книг и фильмов.

A **damsel** in distress is the classical plot of many books and movies.

1841 - Временный ['vremennyj] - *Temporary*

Говорят, что это ограничение носит **временный** характер, но я не верю этому.

They say this restriction is of a **temporary** nature, but I don't believe it.

1842 - Составить [sas'tavit'] - To constitute, to comprise; to construct (perfective)

Местные компании должны **составить** ядро будущей организации.

The local companies must **constitute** the core of the future organisation.

1843 - Ровно ['rovnə] - Sharp, exactly; smoothly, evenly

Я заеду за тобой **ровно** в шесть. Будь готова к этому времени.

I'll pick you up at six **sharp**. Be ready by this time.

1844 - Мечта [metch'ta] - *A dream*

Дом у океана – это моя **мечта**. Я делаю всё возможное, чтобы её осуществить.

A house by the ocean is my **dream**. I'm doing everything possible to make it come true.

1845 - Кольцо [kal''tso] - *A ring*

Это золотое **кольцо** дорого мне как память о бабушке.

This golden **ring** is dear to me as a memory of my grandmother.

1846 - Ага [a'ga] - Yep, yeah (colloquial for 'yes')

Ага, хорошо. Обязательно зайду к тебе, когда будет время.
Yep, alright. I'll surely drop by if I have time.

1847 - Дочка ['dotchka] - A daughter (diminutive or colloquial for 'дочь' [dotch'])

Я не могу поверить, что наша маленькая **дочка** уже выросла.
I can't believe our little **daughter** has grown up already.

1848 - Королева [kara'leva] - *A queen*

Английская **королева** обладает только номинальной властью.
The English **Queen** has only nominal power.

1849 - Картошка [kar'toshka] - *Potatoes (colloquial)*

На ужин у нас жареная **картошка** и овощной салат.
We have fried **potatoes** and a vegetable salad for supper.

1850 - Достоинство [das'toinstvə] - *Dignity*

Я не собираюсь терять своё **достоинство** и умолять их взять меня обратно на работу.
I'm not going to lose my **dignity** and beg them to take me back to work.

1851 - Медведь [med'ved'] - *A bear*

Медведь – популярный персонаж русских сказок.
The **bear** is a popular character of Russian fairy tales.

1852 - Содержание [sader'zhanije] - *Content; maintenance*

Меня интересует **содержание** этого курса. Может, стоит на него подписаться?
I'm interested in the **content** of this course. Maybe it's worth signing up for it.

1853 - Проект [pra'ekt] - *A project*

Можно мне взглянуть на **проект** здания? Я хочу убедиться, что всё в порядке.

May I have a look at the **project** of the building? I want to make sure everything is alright.

1854 - Обида [a'bida] - *A grudge, an insult*

Твой отказ приехать – это *личная* **обида** *для меня*.

Your refusal to come is a personal **insult** for me.

1855 - Согласен [sag'lasen] - **To agree (part of a predicative construction, the initial form is for a masculine or neuter subject)**

Он **согласен** со всем, что говорят другие. У него нет своего мнения.

He **agrees** with everything others say. He doesn't have his own opinion.

1856 - Покупать [paku'pat'] - *To buy*

Я *люблю* **покупать** вещи онлайн. Никакой суеты и тяжёлых сумок.

I like **to buy** things online. No fuss and heavy bags.

1857 - Сперва [sper'va] - **First, at first, firstly (more typical for literary style)**

Сперва помой руки, а потом садись за стол.

Wash your hands **first** and then sit at the table.

1858 - Юный ['junyj] - **Young, youthful (in especially young, teenage years)**

Он такой **юный** и наивный и совсем не знает жизни.

He's so **young** and naive and doesn't know life at all.

1859 - Любопытство [lʼubaˈpytstva] - *Curiosity*

Её **любопытство** раздражает меня! Она хочет знать всё обо всех в мельчайших деталях.

Her **curiosity** irritates me! She wants to know everything about everybody in smallest detail.

1860 - Создание [sazˈdanije] - *Creation; a creature*

Создание такой информационной базы может занять годы.

The **creation** of such a database may take years.

1861 - Паспорт [ˈpaspart] - *A passport*

Только не говори мне, что ты забыла свой **паспорт** дома. Тебя не пустят на борт.

Just don't tell me you left your **passport** at home. They won't let you on board.

1862 - Двести [ˈdvesti] - *Two hundred*

Мне предложили на **двести** долларов больше, если я закончу работу раньше.

I was offered an extra **two hundred** dollars if I finish the work earlier.

1863 - Коллега [kaˈlega] - *A colleague*

Мой **коллега** на больничном, и мне приходится работать за двоих.

My **colleague** is on a sick leave and I have to work for both of us.

1864 - Девчонка [devˈtchjonka] - *A girl, a gal (colloquial)*

Моя племянница – милая, активная **девчонка**.

My niece is a nice and active **girl**.

1865 - Луч [lutch'] - *A ray, a beam*

Котёнок бегал по комнате, пытаясь поймать **луч** света.

A kitten was running about the room trying to catch a light **ray**.

1866 - Стучать [stu'tchat'] - *To knock*

Тебя не учили **стучать** в дверь? Это моя комната, моё пространство.

Haven't you been taught how **to knock** on the door? It's my room, my space.

1867 - Коммунист [kamu'nist] - A communist (person who follows a communist or Marxist-Leninist philosophy)

Мой дедушка – убеждённый **коммунист**. Спорить с ним бесполезно.

My granddad is a convinced **communist**. It's no use arguing with him.

1868 - Просьба ['pros'ba] - *A request*

Твоя **просьба** неуместна. Я не могу помогать тебе бесконечно.

Your **request** is inappropriate. I can't help you endlessly.

1869 - Домик ['domik] - A cottage, a little house

У моих друзей есть **домик** в лесу. Идеальное место, чтобы отдохнуть от суеты города.

My friends have **a cottage** in the forest. A perfect place to rest from the fuss of the city.

1870 - Полчаса [poltcha'sa] - *Half an hour*

Я немного занята сейчас. Перезвоню тебе через **полчаса**.

I'm a bit busy now. I'll call you back in **half an hour**.

1871 - Железо [zhe'leza] - *Iron*

Железо – один из важнейших элементов для правильного обмена веществ.

Iron is one of the most important elements for a proper metabolism.

1872 - Отличие [at'litchije] - *A difference; a distinction*

Смотри, какая интересная головоломка. Найди одно **отличие** между этими картинками.

Look what an interesting puzzle. Find one **difference** between these pictures.

1873 - Менять [men''at'] - *To change; to replace*

Я ничего не хочу **менять** в своей жизни. Я абсолютно счастлив.

I don't want **to change** anything in my life. I'm absolutely happy.

1874 - Мгновенно [mgna'venna] - *Instantly, immediately*

При ограблении сигнализация сработала **мгновенно**.

During the robbery the alarm went off **instantly**.

1875 - Пёс [p'os] - A dog, a hound (male)

Мой преданный **пёс** всегда встречает меня радостным лаем, когда я возвращаюсь с работы.

My loyal **dog** always greets me with joyful barking when I'm returning home from work.

1876 - Разглядывать [raz'gljadyvat'] - To look at, to examine (to look at attentively trying to find something or just paying attention to detail)

Мне нравится **разглядывать** насекомых под лупой.

I like **to look at** insects under the magnifying glass.

1877 - Горький ['gor'kij] - Bitter (both figuratively and literally)

Я не понимаю, как людям может нравится **горький** шоколад.

I don't understand how people can like **bitter** chocolate.

1878 - Орудие [a'rudije] - A tool (both literally and figuratively)

Ты не понимаешь: ты всего лишь **орудие** в её хитрой игре.

You don't understand: you're just **a tool** in her cunning game.

1879 - Специально [spetsi'al'nə] - *Specially; on purpose*

Ты знаешь, я не люблю виноград. Я купила его **специально** для тебя.

You know, I don't like grapes. I bought them **specially** for you.

1880 - Сказка ['skaska] - *A fairy tale, a tale*

Когда я была маленькой девочкой, мне очень нравилась **сказка** про Белоснежку.

When I was a little girl I liked the **fairy tale** about Snow White a lot.

1881 - Закурить [zaku'rit'] - To smoke (to start smoking a cigarette) (perfective)

Можно мне **закурить** прямо здесь? Или мне лучше выйти на улицу?

May I **smoke** right here? Or should I better go outside?

1882 - Семейный [se'mejnyj] - *Family (adj)*

В субботу у нас будет большой **семейный** ужин, так я что не пойду с вами.

On Saturday we're having a big **family** supper, so I'm not going with you.

1883 - Устать [us'tat'] - *To get tired (perfective)*

Как ты мог так быстро **устать**? Мы прошли всего пару километров.

How could you **get tired** so soon? We've just walked a few kilometers.

1884 - Прикрыть [prik'ryt'] - To close, to shut (softly and not completely); to cover up

Я уложила ребёнка спать, но забыла **прикрыть** дверь, и шум голосов разбудил его.

I put the baby to sleep but forgot **to close** the door and the noise of voices woke him up.

1885 - Твёрдо ['tv'ordə] - Firmly (both literally and figuratively, decisively, resolutely)

Я **твёрдо** верю в то, что все перемены в жизни к лучшему.

I **firmly** believe that all the changes in life are for the better.

1886 - Молодец [mala'dets] - *Well done*

Отличный бросок! **Молодец**!

Nice throw! **Well done**!

1887 - Замолчать [zamal'tchat'] - To become/fall silent (to stop talking) (perfective)

Она отвергла все мои аргументы, и я решила, что мне лучше **замолчать**.

She rejected all my arguments and I decided I'd better **become silent**.

1888 - Завести [zaves'ti] - To have (to start having, like a family, child, a pet) (perfective)

Я хочу **завести** домашнего питомца, но не могу выбрать между кошкой и собакой.

I want **to have** a pet but can't choose between a cat and a dog.

1889 - Прибыть [pri'byt'] - *To arrive*

Поезд должен был **прибыть** полчаса назад. Что могло случиться?

The train was **to arrive** half an hour ago. What could have happened?

1890 - Собрание [sa'branije] - A meeting, a gathering; a collection

Обязательно посети завтрашнее **собрание**. Там будут обсуждаться важные вопросы.

Be sure to attend tomorrow's **meeting**. They are going to discuss important matters there.

1891 - Девять ['dev'at'] - *Nine*

В этом сервизе десять тарелок. Я вижу только **девять**.

There are ten plates in this dining set. I see only **nine**.

1892 - Слон [slon] - *An elephant*

Слон обладает феноменальной памятью.

The **elephant** has a phenomenal memory.

1893 - Подтвердить [pattver'dit'] - *To confirm*

Вам нужно **подтвердить** это действие, прежде чем вы перейдёте к следующему.

You need **to confirm** this action before you go over to the next one.

1894 - Юноша ['junasha] - A youth (male), a young man

Этот **юноша** талантлив, но недостаточно трудолюбив.

This **youth** is talented but not hard working enough.

1895 - Сойти [saj'ti] - To go off; to go down (perfective)

Дай я помогу тебе **сойти** с автобуса. Здесь рядом большая лужа.

Let me help you **get off** the bus. There's a big puddle near here.

1896 - Поступать [pastu'pat'] - To act, to behave; to enter, to join

Ты уже не ребёнок. Тебе нужно научиться **поступать** мудрее.

You're not a child anymore. You must learn **to act** more wisely.

1897 - Крутой [kru'toj] - Steep; cool, awesome (colloquial)

Там впереди **крутой** спуск. Я думаю, нам лучше сойти с велосипедов и пройти пешком.

There's a **steep** slope ahead. I think we'd better get off the bikes and go on foot.

1898 - Валить [va'lit'] - To blame (to put the blame on somebody else)

Не надо **валить** всё на меня! Ты тоже был там!

Don't **blame** everything on me! You were there too!

1899 - Объект [ab'jekt] - *An object*

Вчера я видел в небе странный **объект**. Надеюсь, это были инопланетяне.

Yesterday I saw a strange **object** in the sky. I hope those were extraterrestrials.

1900 - Убитый [u'bityj] - *Murdered, killed*

Мужчина, **убитый** в собственном доме, был найден только через три дня.

The man, **murdered** in his own house, was found only after three days.

1901 - Сравнение [srav'nenije] - *A comparison*

Сравнение с животными или предметами иногда помогает писателям лучше описать героя.

A comparison with animals or objects sometimes helps writers to describe a character better.

1902 - Справа ['sprava] - *On the right, to the right*

Пожалуйста, принеси лимонад. Он возле микроволновки, **справа**.

Please, fetch the lemonade. It's next to the microwave, **on the right**.

1903 - Благородный [blaga'rodnyj] - *Noble*

Ты правильно сделал, что не взял деньги обратно. Это был благородный **поступок**.

You did right not taking the money back. That was a **noble** deed.

1904 - Океан [ake'an] - *An ocean*

Тихий **океан** самый большой и самый глубокий **океан** в мире.

The Pacific **Ocean** is the largest and the deepest **ocean** in the world.

1905 - Посёлок [pa's'olək] - A village (usually a big one); a settlement

К утру весь **посёлок** знал о вчерашней драке.

By the morning the whole **village** knew about yesterday's fight.

1906 - Тайга [taj'ga] - *Taiga*

Тайга – это хвойные леса, которые простираются на тысячи километров.

Taiga are coniferous forests that stretch for thousands of kilometers.

1907 - Борода [bara'da] - *A beard*

Мне нравится моя **борода**. Мне кажется, она придаёт мне брутальный вид.

I like my **beard**. It seems to me it makes me look more masculine.

1908 - Пачка ['patchka] - *A pack, a package*

Эта **пачка** сигарет была в твоём кармане. Ты куришь?

This **pack** of cigarettes was in your pocket. Do you smoke?

1909 - Надоесть [nada'jest'] - To get tired of, to get bored by (impersonal, the person who's tired/bored takes the dative case)

Как тебе могла **надоесть** эта песня? Я готова слушать её снова и снова.

How could you **get tired of** this song? I'm ready to listen to it over and over again.

1910 - Привычка [pri'vytchka] - *A habit*

Я знаю, что есть по ночам, – это плохая **привычка**, но не могу от неё избавиться.

I know that eating at night is a bad **habit** but I can't get rid of it.

1911 - Сумма ['suma] - *A sum*

Вчера из местного банка была украдена крупная **сумма** денег.

A large **sum** of money was stolen from the local bank yesterday.

1912 - Вывести ['vyvesti] - To lead (out of); to withdraw

Девочка смогла **вывести** младшего брата из горящего дома.

The girl managed **to lead** her younger brother out of the burning house.

1913 - Прыгать ['prygat'] - *To jump, to leap*

Ты будешь **прыгать** от радости, когда увидишь наш новый дом.

You're going **to jump** with joy when you see our new house.

1914 - Создавать [sazda'vat'] - *To create*

Мы будем **создавать** все необходимые условия для улучшения качества образования.

We're going **to create** all the necessary conditions to improve the quality of education.

1915 - Грубый ['grubyj] - *Rude; rough*

Я не понимаю, почему он такой **грубый** сегодня. Обычно он очень вежливый.

I don't understand why he's so **rude** today. Usually he's very polite.

1916 - Поездка [pa'jestka] - *A trip*

Это будет замечательная **поездка**! Мы посетим две страны и пять городов.

It's going to be a wonderful **trip**! We'll visit two countries and five cities.

1917 - Убедиться [ube'ditsa] - *To make sure (perfective)*

Подожди минуточку. Я хочу **убедиться**, что выключила утюг.

Wait a minute. I want **to make sure** I've switched off the iron.

1918 - Ненавидеть [nena'videt'] - *To hate*

Я не понимаю, как можно **ненавидеть** человека, которого ты когда-то любил.

I don't understand how it's possible **to hate** a person you used to love.

1919 - Заявление [zajav'lenije] - *An application; a statement*

Мы рассмотрим ваше **заявление** в течение этой недели.
We'll consider your **application** within this week.

1920 - Поражение [para'zhenie] - *A defeat*

Он не может пережить своё **поражение** на шахматном турнире.
He can't live over his **defeat** at the chess tournament.

1921 - Август ['avgust] - *August*

Август мой самый нелюбимый месяц. Он напоминает мне, что скоро осень.
August is my least favorite month. It reminds me that soon there will be autumn.

1922 - Привычный [pri'vytchnyj] - *Habitual, customary*

Я не люблю, когда что-нибудь вмешивается в мой **привычный** ритм жизни.
I don't like it when something interferes with my **habitual** pace of life.

1923 - Официально [afitsi'alnə] - *Officially*

Поздравьте нас! Теперь мы **официально** женаты.
Congratulate us! We're **officially** married now.

1924 - Передний [pe'rednij] - *Front, fore*

Просторный **передний** двор – одно из главных преимуществ этого дома.
A spacious **front** yard is one of the major advantages of this house.

1925 - Север ['sever] - *North*

Я думаю, что если мы пойдём на **север**, то скоро выйдем из леса.

I think if we go **north**, we'll go out of the forest soon.

1926 - Шляпа ['shl'apa] - *A hat (with brims)*

Эта **шляпа** отлично дополнит твой деловой образ.

This **hat** will greatly compliment your business look.

1927 - Изо ['izə] - From, out of (a form of 'из' used before consonant clusters)

На карнавал в Рио приезжают люди **изо** всех уголков мира.

People **from** all the corners of the world come to the Rio Carnival.

1928 - Молчание [mal'tchanije] - Silence (the quiet because of the absence of speech)

Молчание становилось неловким, но никто не знал, как прервать его.

The **silence** was getting awkward but nobody knew how to break it.

1929 - Исчезать [istche'zat'] - *To disappear, to vanish*

Нельзя вот так **исчезать**, не предупредив никого. Мы волновались.

You can't **disappear** like that without warning anyone. We were worried.

1930 - Эй [ɛj] - *Hey*

Эй, ты! Подойди сюда!

Hey, you there! Come here!

1931 - Топор [ta'por] - *An axe*

В музее мы увидели боевой **топор** викингов.
We saw a battle **axe** of the Vikings in the museum.

1932 - Ощущать [astchust'chat'] - *To feel, to sense*

Это удивительно, как я могу **ощущать** твою поддержку даже на расстоянии.
It's amazing how I can **feel** your support even at a distance.

1933 - Тащить [tast'chit'] - *To drag, to pull*

Сумка была такой тяжёлой, что я не могла нести её и мне пришлось **тащить** её.
The bag was so heavy that I couldn't carry it and had to **drag** it.

1934 - Брюки ['br'uki] - Trousers (more for formal, business style)

Дай мне салфетку, пожалуйста. Я пролил сок на **брюки**.
Give me a napkin, please. I've spilled some juice on my **trousers**.

1935 - Соответствующий [saat'vetstvujustchij] - *Corresponding, respective*

Я не думаю, что получу работу. У меня отсутствует **соответствующий** опыт.
I don't think I'll get the job. I don't have the **corresponding** experience.

1936 - Элемент [ɛle'ment] - An element, a component; an item

Этот крошечный **элемент** оборудования играет очень важную роль в его работе.
This tiny **element** of the equipment plays a very important role in its work.

1937 - Одеяло [adeˈjalə] - *A blanket*

Пора доставать тёплое **одеяло**. Я замёрзла прошлой ночью.
It's time to take out a warm **blanket**. I was freezing last night.

1938 - Мотор [maˈtor] - *An engine, a motor*

Мотор моей машины издаёт какие-то странные звуки. Мне нужно показать его механику.
My car's **engine** is giving out some strange sounds. I need to take it to a mechanic.

1939 - Везде [vezˈde] - *Everywhere, anywhere*

Я искала твои бумаги **везде**. Ты уверена, что оставила их у меня дома?
I've been looking for your papers **everywhere**. Are you sure you left them at my place?

1940 - Дружба [ˈdruzhba] - *Friendship*

Со временем наша **дружба** стала ещё сильнее.
With time our **friendship** got even stronger.

1941 - Безопасность [bezaˈpasnəstʼ] - *Security, safety*

Государство обязано обеспечивать **безопасность** своих граждан.
The state is obliged to ensure the **security** of its citizens.

1942 - Скрывать [skryˈvatʼ] - *To hide, to conceal*

Супруги не должны ничего **скрывать** друг от друга. У них не должно быть никаких секретов.
Spouses shouldn't **hide** anything from each other. They shouldn't have any secrets.

1943 - Совершить [saver'shit'] - To commit, to perform (perfective)

Я не верю, что он мог **совершить** это ужасное преступление! Это совсем на него не похоже!

I don't believe he could **commit** that terrible crime! It's absolutely unlike him.

1944 - Крест [krest] - *A cross*

Крест – это центральный символ христианской религии.

The **cross** is the central symbol of the Christian religion.

1945 - Земной [zem'noj] - Earthly, earth (adj), terrestrial

Наш **земной** мир не совершенен, но есть надежда, что небесный сильно от него отличается.

Our **earthly** world is not perfect but there's hope that the heavenly one differs from it a lot.

1946 - Школьный ['shkol'nyj] - *School (adj)*

Я опоздал на **школьный** автобус, и маме пришлось везти меня в школу на машине.

I missed the **school** bus and Mom had to take me to school by car.

1947 - Замереть [zame'ret'] - To freeze, to stand motionless (perfective)

Это простая игра. Как только я скажу волшебные слова, вы должны **замереть**.

It's a simple game. As soon as I say the magic words you must **freeze**.

1948 - Прозрачный [praz'rachnyj] - *Transparent, clear*

Бульон для этого супа должен быть **прозрачный**, а твой мутный и тёмный.

The broth for this soup must be **transparent** and yours is cloudy and dark.

1949 - Подавать [pada'vat'] - **To give (means to give something to someone who's far from the object)**

Малыш, я больше не буду **подавать** тебе игрушки, которые ты нарочно сбрасываешь на пол.

Baby I'm not going **to give** you the toys your're dropping on the floor on purpose.

1950 - Истинный ['istinyj] - *True; genuine*

Он **истинный** фанат футбола. Он знает всё обо всех командах и их игроках.

He's **a true** football fan. He knows everything about all teams and their players.

1951 - Кабина [ka'bina] - *A cab, a cabin*

В моём новом грузовике очень удобная **кабина**: мягкие сиденья, кондиционер.

My new truck has a very comfortable **cab**: soft seats, an air conditioner.

1952 - Пальто [pal''to] - *A coat, an overcoat*

Я коплю деньги на новое **пальто** из дизайнерской коллекции.

I'm saving up money for a new **coat** from a designer collection.

1953 - Восторг [vas'torg] - *Delight, ecstasy*

Тебе нужно было видеть его **восторг**, когда он увидел, что мне удалось купить билеты.

You should have seen his **delight** when he saw that I had managed to buy the tickets.

1954 - Экономика [ɛka'nomika] - *Economy; economics*

Рыночная **экономика** не может развиваться в жёстких рамках.

Market **economy** can't develop in a rigid framework.

1955 - Забота [za'bota] - *Care*

Материнская **забота** – это вещь, которую ничем нельзя заменить.

Mother's **care** can't be replaced with anything.

1956 - Произвести [praizves'ti] - *To produce (perfective)*

В этом году наш завод планирует **произвести** в два раза больше товаров, чем в прошлом году.

This year our factory is planning **to produce** twice as many goods as in the previous year.

1957 - Дождаться [dazh'datsa] - To wait (to wait for a long time and finally get what you've been waiting for), (perfective)

Я не могу **дождаться**, когда впервые увижу моего новорождённого племянника.

I can't **wait** to see my newborn nephew for the first time.

1958 - Талант [ta'lant] - *A talent, a gift*

У него настоящий **талант** к рисованию. Отправьте его в художественную школу.

He has a real **talent** for painting. Send him to an art school.

1959 - Плыть [plyt'] - *To swim*

Не пытайся **плыть** против течения. Ты недостаточно силён для этого.

Don't try **to swim** against the current. You're not strong enough for it.

1960 - Запись ['zapis'] - *A recording (of a voice or a sound); an entry*

Послушайте эту **запись**. Вы узнаёте этот голос?

Listen to this **recording**. Do you recognize this voice?

1961 - Ведро [ved'ro] - *A bucket*

Она взяла **ведро** с водой и швабру и принялась за уборку.

She took a **bucket** with water and a mop and got down to work.

1962 - Крестьянин [krest''janin] - *A peasant*

Не каждый **крестьянин** в те времена мог позволить себе такой большой дом.

Not every **peasant** in those times could afford such a big house.

1963 - Поворот [pava'rot] - *A turning; a turn*

Я ехала слишком быстро и пропустила свой **поворот**.

I was driving too fast and missed my **turning**.

1964 - Подробность [pad'robnəst'] - *A detail, a particularity*

Как прошло твоё свидание? Я хочу знать каждую **подробность**.

How did your date go? I want to know every **detail**.

1965 - Столб [stolp] - *A post, a pole*

Посмотри, этот заборный **столб** сгнил. Нам нужно заменить его.

Look, this fence **post** is rotten. We need to replace it.

1966 - Канал [ka'nal] - *A channel; a canal*

Переключи на новостной **канал**. Мне интересно, что происходит в мире.

Switch to the news **channel**. I wonder what's going on in the world.

1967 - Пассажир [pasa'zhyr] - *A passenger*

Каждый **пассажир** самолёта должен иметь действительный паспорт.

Every **passenger** of a plane must have a valid passport.

1968 - Выполнить ['vypəlnit'] - *To carry out, to fulfill (perfective)*

Вы должны **выполнить** свои обязательства, иначе мы разорвём контракт.

You must **carry out** your obligations, otherwise we'll break the contract.

1969 - Устройство [ust'rojstvə] - *A device*

Это простое **устройство** позволяет измерять пульс и кровяное давление.

This simple **device** allows you to measure the pulse and the blood pressure.

1970 - Благодаря [blagada'r'a] - *Thanks to, due to*

Благодаря поддержке родителей и друзей, мне удалось построить впечатляющую карьеру.

Thanks to the support of my parents and friends I managed to build an impressive career.

1971 - Направиться [nap'ravitsa] - *To head (reflexive), (perfective)*

Я советую тебе отложить все дела и **направиться** в горы или к морю.

I advise you to put away all your business and **head** to the mountains or to the seaside.

1972 - Влияние [vli'janije] - *Influence*

Нельзя недооценивать **влияние** общества на формирование личности ребёнка.

One can't underestimate the **influence** of society on the development of a child's personality.

1973 - Ракета [ra'keta] - *A rocket*

Ракета ещё не полностью готова. Нам придётся отложить запуск.

The **rocket** is not completely ready yet. We'll have to delay the launch.

1974 - Гражданский [grazh'danskij] - *Civil, civic*

Участие в выборах – это мой **гражданский** долг.

The participation in the elections is my **civil** duty.

1975 - Шутить [shu'tit'] - *To joke; to make fun (of)*

Она совсем не умеет **шутить**. Мне никогда не нравилось её чувство юмора.

She's absolutely unable **to joke**. I've never liked her sense of humor.

1976 - Смена ['smena] - *A change, replacement; a shift*

Смена правительства должна происходить раз в четыре года.

The **change** of government must take place once in four years.

1977 - Случаться [slu'tchatsa] - *To happen, to occur*

Неудачи должны **случаться**. Они делают нас сильнее.
Misfortunes should **happen**. They make us stronger.

1978 - Спрятать ['spr'atat'] - To hide (perfective, transitive)

Я могу так хорошо **спрятать** эти деньги, что никто никогда их не найдёт.
I can **hide** this money so well that nobody will ever find it.

1979 - Предстоит [predsta'it] - Impersonal for 'To be to', 'To have to', means that the person has something ahead, the subject takes the dative case.

Я хочу больше узнать об этом городе, раз мне **предстоит** жить в нём.
I want to learn more about this city if I **am to** live in it.

1980 - Затылок [za'tylək] - *Back of the head, nape*

Он почесал **затылок**, думая, как ответить на мой вопрос.
He scratched the **back of his head** thinking how to answer my question.

1981 - Юг [jug] - *South*

Летом мы собираемся поехать на **юг** и отдохнуть у моря.
In summer we're planning to go to the **south** and have a rest at the seaside.

1982 - Эпоха [ε'poha] – An era, an age, an epoche

Каждая историческая **эпоха** имела свои ценности и идеалы.
Every historical *era* had its values and ideals.

1983 - Товар [ta'var] - Goods (unlike in English has a singular form), a product

Покупатель заранее оплатил **товар** и его доставку.
The buyer paid for the **product** and its delivery in advance.

1984 - Проклятый ['prokl'atyj] - *Cursed*

Это **проклятый** замок, и только настоящая любовь может разрушить заклятье.
It's a **cursed** castle and only true love can break the spell.

1985 - Ветка ['vetka] - A twig, a branch; a branch line

Тонкая **ветка** ударила меня по лицу и оставила красный след.
A thin **twig** hit me in the face and left a red mark.

1986 - Кормить [kar'mit'] - *To feed*

Животных в зоопарке **кормить** запрещено.
It's forbidden **to feed** animals in the zoo.

1987 - Продолжаться [pradal'zhatsa] - *To last, to continue*

Обучение в университете будет **продолжаться** четыре года.
The university study will **last** four years.

1988 - Разведчик [raz'vetchik] - *An intelligence officer*

Этот **разведчик** – герой гражданской войны.
This **intelligence officer** is a hero of The Civil War.

1989 - Отлично [at'litchnə] - *Great*

Хорошо, **отлично**, встретимся у кинотеатра в пять.
Alright, **great**, we'll meet outside the cinema at five.

1990 - Боже ['bozhe] - *God, Lord*

О, **Боже**! Я не сохранила документ и придётся начинать сначала.

Oh, **God**! I didn't save the document and I'll have to start all over again.

1991 - Молодость ['moladast'] - *Youth*

В этом городе я провёл свою **молодость**, поэтому я люблю возвращаться сюда.

I spent my **youth** in this city and that is why I like to return here.

1992 - Отдыхать [atdy'hat'] - *To rest, to have rest*

Тебе нужно больше **отдыхать**. Ты слишком много работаешь.

You need **to rest** more. You work too much.

1993 - Октябрь [ak't'abr'] - *October*

Я точно помню. Это был **октябрь**.

I remember it for sure. That was **October**.

1994 - Широко [shira'ko] - *Widely, wide (adv)*

Это **широко** известный производитель кожаной обуви и сумок.

It's a **widely** known producer of leather footwear and bags.

1995 - Храм [hram] - A church, a cathedral (more elevated style); a temple

По воскресеньям мы ходим в **храм**.

On Sundays we go to **church**.

1996 - Сдать [zdat'] - *To hand in (perfective)*

Учитель сказал ученикам **сдать** сочинения к четвергу.

The teacher told the pupils **to hand in** their essays by Thursday.

1997 - Шестой [shes'toj] - *Sixth*

Ты ешь уже **шестой** кекс. Остановись!
It's the **sixth** muffin you're eating. Stop!

1998 - Жаловаться ['zhalavats'a] - *To complain*

Я буду **жаловаться** на ваш сервис!
I'm going **to complain** about your service!

1999 - Скала [ska'la] - *A rock, a cliff*

Нам нужно развернуть корабль. Впереди **скала**!
We need to turn the ship around. There is a **rock** ahead!

2000 - Расчёт [ras'tchjot] - *Calculation, computation*

Я не смогу произвести такой сложный **расчёт** без
специальной формулы.
I won't be able to carry out such a complex **calculation** without a
special formula.

CONCLUSION

And thus, we've finally reached the very end of this wonderful list of the 2000 Most Common Words in Russian! Be glad: your vocabulary has been greatly increased, and, as we mentioned before, if you've properly studied these words, then you will have developed your understanding of non-fiction to 84%, your fiction to 86.1%, and your oral speech to 92.7%. Those are incredible numbers, considering how important the understanding of vocabulary is when learning a new language and using that to communicate in new languages and with different cultures.

While you've been studying this great list, you may have noticed the similarities and differences between our beloved English and the Russian language – the major difference is in the abundance of endings in different word forms. But, again don't be discouraged by this fact. The long way to Fuji starts with the first step, and you've made at least two thousand!

If you feel you've made progress in Russian, we're happy to have helped you and hope to see you again soon; we'll surely meet again in future books and learning material.

So, take care and study hard, and don't forget the 4 tips we gave you at the beginning if you want to become a pro in Russian!

- Practice hard!
- Don't limit yourself to these 2000 words!
- Grab a study partner!
- Write a story!

With that said, we've covered every single thing. Now go out and learn some more Russian – you're already more than halfway there!

PS: Keep an eye out for more books like this one; we're not done teaching you Russian! Head over to www.LingoMastery.com and read our free articles, sign up for our newsletter and check out our Youtube channel. We give away so much free stuff that will accelerate your Russian learning and you don't want to miss that!

If you liked the book, we would really appreciate a little review wherever you bought it.

THANKS FOR READING!

Made in United States
Orlando, FL
13 February 2023

29951251R00163